THE DYNAMICS CAPITAL

ARVIND UPADHYAY

The distribution of wealth is one of today's most widely discussed and controversial issues. But what do we really know about its evolution over the long term? Do the dynamics of private capital accumulation inevitably lead to the concentration of wealth in ever fewer hands, as Karl Marx believed in the nineteenth century? Or do the balancing forces of growth, competition, and technological progress lead in later stages of development to reduced inequality and greater harmony among the classes, as Simon Kuznets thought in the twentieth century? What do we really know about how wealth and income have evolved since the eighteenth century, and what lessons can we derive from that knowledge for the century now under way? These are the questions I attempt to answer in this book. Let me say at once that the answers contained herein are imperfect and incomplete. But they are based on much more extensive historical and comparative data than were available to previous researchers, data covering three centuries and more than twenty countries, as well as on a new theoretical framework that affords a deeper understanding of the underlying mechanisms. Modern economic growth and the diffusion of knowledge have made it possible to avoid the Marxist apocalypse but have not modified the deep structures of capital and inequality—or in any case not as much as one might have imagined in the optimistic decades following World War II. When the rate of return on capital exceeds the rate of growth of output and income, as it did in the nineteenth century and seems quite likely to do again in the twenty-first, capitalism automatically generates arbitrary and unsustainable inequalities that radically undermine the meritocratic values on which democratic societies are based. There are nevertheless ways democracy can regain control over capitalism and ensure that the general interest takes precedence over private interests, while preserving economic openness and avoiding protectionist and nationalist reactions. The policy recommendations I propose later in the book tend in this direction. They are based on lessons derived from historical experience, of which what follows is essentially a narrative.Intellectual and political debate about the distribution of wealth has long been based on an abundance of prejudice and a paucity of fact. To be sure, it would be a mistake to underestimate the importance of the intuitive knowledge that everyone acquires about contemporary wealth and income levels, even in the absence of any theoretical framework or statistical analysis. Film and literature, nineteenth-century novels especially, are full of detailed information about the relative wealth and living standards of different social groups, and especially about the deep structure of inequality, the way it is justified, and its impact on individual lives. Indeed, the novels of Jane Austen and Honoré de Balzac paint striking portraits of the distribution of wealth in Britain and France between 1790 and 1830. Both novelists were intimately acquainted with the hierarchy of wealth in their respective societies. They grasped the hidden contours of wealth and its inevitable implications for the lives of men and women, including their marital strategies and personal hopes and disappointments. These and other novelists depicted the effects of inequality with a verisimilitude and evocative power that no statistical or theoretical analysis can match. Indeed, the distribution of wealth is too important an issue to be left to economists, sociologists, historians, and philosophers. It is of interest to everyone, and that is a good thing. The concrete, physical reality of inequality is visible to the naked eye and naturally inspires sharp but contradictory political judgments. Peasant and noble, worker and factory owner, waiter and banker: each has his or her own unique vantage point and sees important aspects of how other people live and what relations of power and domination exist between social groups, and these observations shape each person's judgment of what is and is not just. Hence there will always be a fundamentally subjective and psychological dimension to inequality, which inevitably gives rise to political conflict that no purportedly scientific analysis can alleviate. Democracy will never be supplanted by a republic of experts—and that is a very good thing. Nevertheless, the distribution question also deserves to be studied in a systematic and methodical fashion. Without precisely defined sources, methods, and concepts, it is possible to see everything and its opposite. Some people believe that inequality is always increasing and that the world is by definition always becoming more unjust. Others believe that inequality is naturally decreasing, or that harmony comes about automatically, and that in any case nothing should be done that might risk disturbing this happy equilibrium. Given this dialogue of the deaf, in which each camp justifies its own intellectual laziness by pointing to the laziness of the other, there is a role for research that is at least systematic and methodical if not fully scientific. Expert analysis will never put an end to the violent political conflict that inequality inevitably instigates. Social scientific research is and always will be tentative and imperfect. It does not claim to transform economics, sociology, and history into exact sciences. But by patiently searching for facts and patterns and calmly analyzing the economic, social, and political mechanisms that might explain them, it can inform democratic debate and focus attention on the right questions. It can help to redefine the terms of debate, unmask certain preconceived or fraudulent notions, and subject all positions to constant critical scrutiny. In my view, this is the role that intellectuals, including social scientists, should play, as citizens like any other but with the good fortune to have more time than others to devote themselves to study (and even to be paid for it—a signal privilege). There is no escaping the fact, however, that social science research on the distribution of wealth was for a long time based on a relatively limited set of firmly established facts together with a wide variety of purely theoretical speculations. Before turning in greater detail to the sources I tried to assemble in preparation for writing this book, I want to give a quick historical overview of previous thinking about these issues. Malthus, Young, and the French Revolution When classical political economy was born in England and France in the late eighteenth and early nineteenth century, the issue of distribution was already one of the key questions. Everyone realized that radical transformations were under way, precipitated by sustained demographic growth—a previously unknown phenomenon—coupled with a rural exodus and the advent of the Industrial Revolution. How would these upheavals affect the distribution of wealth, the social structure, and the political equilibrium of European society? For Thomas Malthus, who in 1798 published his Essay on the Principle of Population, there could be no doubt: the primary threat was overpopulation. Although his sources were thin, he made the best he could of them. One particularly important influence was the travel diary published by Arthur Young, an English agronomist who traveled extensively in France, from Calais to the Pyrenees and from Brittany to Franche-Comté, in 1787–1788, on the eve of the Revolution. Young wrote of the poverty of the French countryside. His vivid essay was by no means totally inaccurate. France at that time was by far the most populous country in Europe and therefore an ideal place to observe. The kingdom could already boast of a population of 20 million in 1700, compared to only 8 million for Great Britain (and 5 million for England alone). The French population increased steadily throughout the eighteenth century, from the end of Louis XIV's reign to the demise of Louis XVI, and by 1780 was close to 30 million. There is every reason to believe that this unprecedentedly rapid population growth contributed to a stagnation of agricultural wages and an increase in land rents in the decades prior to the explosion of 1789. Although this demographic shift was not the sole cause of the French Revolution, it clearly contributed to the growing unpopularity of the aristocracy and the existing political regime. Nevertheless, Young's account, published in 1792, also bears the traces of nationalist prejudice and misleading comparison. The great agronomist found the inns in which he stayed thoroughly disagreeable and disliked the manners of the women who waited on him. Although many of his observations were banal and anecdotal, he believed he could derive universal consequences fromthem. He was mainly worried that the mass poverty he witnessed would lead to political upheaval. In particular, he was convinced that only the English political system, with separate houses of Parliament for aristocrats and commoners and veto power for the nobility, could allow for harmonious and peaceful development led by responsible people. He was convinced that France was headed for ruin when it decided in 1789–1790 to allow both aristocrats and commoners to sit in a single legislative body. It is no exaggeration to say that his whole account was overdetermined by his fear of revolution in France. Whenever one speaks about the distribution of wealth, politics is never very far behind, and it is difficult for anyone to escape contemporary class prejudices and interests. When Reverend Malthus published his famous Essay in 1798, he reached conclusions even more radical than Young's. Like his compatriot, he was very afraid of the new political ideas emanating from France, and to reassure himself that there would be no comparable upheaval in Great Britain he argued that all welfare assistance to the poor must be halted at once and that reproduction by the poor should be severely scrutinized lest the world succumb to overpopulation leading to chaos and misery. It is impossible to understand Malthus's exaggeratedly somber predictions without recognizing the way fear gripped much of the European elite in the 1790s. Ricardo: The Principle of Scarcity 1 In retrospect, it is obviously easy to make fun of these prophecies of doom. It is important to realize, however, that the economic and social transformations of the late eighteenth and early nineteenth centuries were objectively quite impressive, not to say traumatic, for those who witnessed them. Indeed, most contemporary observers—and not only Malthus and Young—shared relatively dark or even apocalyptic views of the long-run evolution of the distribution of wealth and class structure of society. This was true in particular of David Ricardo and Karl Marx, who were surely the two most influential economists of the nineteenth century and who both believed that a small social group—landowners for Ricardo, industrial capitalists for Marx—would inevitably claim a steadily increasing share of output and income. For Ricardo, who published his Principles of Political Economy and Taxation in 1817, the chief concern was the long-term evolution of land prices and land rents. Like Malthus, he had virtually no genuine statistics at his disposal. He nevertheless had intimate knowledge of the capitalism of his time. Born into a family of Jewish financiers with Portuguese roots, he also seems to have had fewer political prejudices than Malthus, Young, or Smith. He was influenced by the Malthusian model but pushed the argument farther. He was above all interested in the following logical paradox. Once both population and output begin to grow steadily, land tends to become increasingly scarce relative to other goods. The law of supply and demand then implies that the price of land will rise continuously, as will the rents paid to landlords. The landlords will therefore claim a growing share of national income, as the share available to the rest of the population decreases, thus upsetting the social equilibrium. For Ricardo, the only logically and politically acceptable answer was to impose a steadily increasing tax on land rents. This somber prediction proved wrong: land rents did remain high for an extended period, but in the end the value of farm land inexorably declined relative to other forms of wealth as the share of agriculture in national income decreased. Writing in the 1810s, Ricardo had no way of anticipating the importance of technological progress or industrial growth in the years ahead. Like Malthus and Young, he could not imagine that humankind would ever be totally freed from the alimentary imperative. His insight into the price of land is nevertheless interesting: the "scarcity principle" on which he relied meant that certain prices might rise to very high levels over many decades. This could well be enough to destabilize entire societies. The price system plays a key role in coordinating the activities of millions of individuals—indeed, today, billions of individuals in the new global economy. The problem is that the price system knows neither limits nor morality. It would be a serious mistake to neglect the importance of the scarcity principle for understanding the global distribution of wealth in the twenty-first century. To convince oneself of this, it is enough to replace the price of farmland in Ricardo's model by the price of urban real estate in major world capitals, or, alternatively, by the price of oil. In both cases, if the trend over the period 1970–2010 is extrapolated to the period 2010–2050 or 2010–2100, the result is economic, social, and political disequilibria of considerable magnitude, not only between but within countries—disequilibria that inevitably call to mind the Ricardian apocalypse. To be sure, there exists in principle a quite simple economic mechanism that should restore equilibrium to the process: the mechanism of supply and demand. If the supply of any good is 2 insufficient, and its price is too high, then demand for that good should decrease, which should lead to a decline in its price. In other words, if real estate and oil prices rise, then people should move to the country or take to traveling about by bicycle (or both). Never mind that such adjustments might be unpleasant or complicated; they might also take decades, during which landlords and oil well owners might well accumulate claims on the rest of the population so extensive that they could easily come to own everything that can be owned, including rural real estate and bicycles, once and for all. As always, the worst is never certain to arrive. It is much too soon to warn readers that by 2050 they may be paying rent to the emir of Qatar. I will consider the matter in due course, and my answer will be more nuanced, albeit only moderately reassuring. But it is important for now to understand that the interplay of supply and demand in no way rules out the possibility of a large and lasting divergence in the distribution of wealth linked to extreme changes in certain relative prices. This is the principal implication of Ricardo's scarcity principle. But nothing obliges us to roll the dice. Marx: The Principle of Infinite Accumulation By the time Marx published the first volume of Capital in 1867, exactly one-half century after the publication of Ricardo's Principles, economic and social realities had changed profoundly: the question was no longer whether farmers could feed a growing population or land prices would rise sky high but rather how to understand the dynamics of industrial capitalism, now in full blossom. The most striking fact of the day was the misery of the industrial proletariat. Despite the growth of the economy, or perhaps in part because of it, and because, as well, of the vast rural exodus owing to both population growth and increasing agricultural productivity, workers crowded into urban slums. The working day was long, and wages were very low. A new urban misery emerged, more visible, more shocking, and in some respects even more extreme than the rural misery of the Old Regime. Germinal, Oliver Twist, and Les Misérables did not spring from the imaginations of their authors, any more than did laws limiting child labor in factories to children older than eight (in France in 1841) or ten in the mines (in Britain in 1842). Dr. Villermé's Tableau de l'état physique et moral des ouvriers employés dans les manufactures, published in France in 1840 (leading to the passage of a timid new child labor law in 1841), described the same sordid reality as The Condition of the Working Class in England, which Friedrich Engels published in 1845. In fact, all the historical data at our disposal today indicate that it was not until the second half—or even the final third—of the nineteenth century that a significant rise in the purchasing power of wages occurred. From the first to the sixth decade of the nineteenth century, workers' wages stagnated at very low levels—close or even inferior to the levels of the eighteenth and previous centuries. This long phase of wage stagnation, which we observe in Britain as well as France, stands out all the more because economic growth was accelerating in this period.

The capital share of national income—industrial profits, land rents, and building rents—insofar as can be estimated with the imperfect sources available today, increased considerably in both countries in the first half of the nineteenth century. It would decrease slightly in the final decades of the nineteenth century, as wages partly caught up with growth. The data we have assembled nevertheless reveal no structural decrease in inequality prior to World War I. What we see in the period 1870–1914 is at best a stabilization of inequality at an extremely high level, and in certain respects an endless inegalitarian spiral, marked in 3 4 5 particular by increasing concentration of wealth. It is quite difficult to say where this trajectory would have led without the major economic and political shocks initiated by the war. With the aid of historical analysis and a little perspective, we can now see those shocks as the only forces since the Industrial Revolution powerful enough to reduce inequality. In any case, capital prospered in the 1840s and industrial profits grew, while labor incomes stagnated. This was obvious to everyone, even though in those days aggregate national statistics did not yet exist. It was in this context that the first communist and socialist movements developed. The central argument was simple: What was the good of industrial development, what was the good of all the technological innovations, toil, and population movements if, after half a century of industrial growth, the condition of the masses was still just as miserable as before, and all lawmakers could do was prohibit factory labor by children under the age of eight? The bankruptcy of the existing economic and political system seemed obvious. People therefore wondered about its long-termevolution: what could one say about it? This was the task Marx set himself. In 1848, on the eve of the "spring of nations" (that is, the revolutions that broke out across Europe that spring), he published The Communist Manifesto, a short, hard-hitting text whose first chapter began with the famous words "A specter is haunting Europe—the specter of communism." The text ended with the equally famous prediction of revolution: "The development of Modern Industry, therefore, cuts from under its feet the very foundation on which the bourgeoisie produces and appropriates products. What the bourgeoisie therefore produces, above all, are its own gravediggers. Its fall and the victory of the proletariat are equally inevitable." Over the next two decades, Marx labored over the voluminous treatise that would justify this conclusion and propose the first scientific analysis of capitalism and its collapse. This work would remain unfinished: the first volume of Capital was published in 1867, but Marx died in 1883 without having completed the two subsequent volumes. His friend Engels published them posthumously after piecing together a text from the sometimes obscure fragments of manuscript Marx had left behind. Like Ricardo, Marx based his work on an analysis of the internal logical contradictions of the capitalist system. He therefore sought to distinguish himself from both bourgeois economists (who saw the market as a self-regulated system, that is, a system capable of achieving equilibrium on its own without major deviations, in accordance with Adam Smith's image of "the invisible hand" and Jean-Baptiste Say's "law" that production creates its own demand), and utopian socialists and Proudhonians, who in Marx's view were content to denounce the misery of the working class without proposing a truly scientific analysis of the economic processes responsible for it. In short, Marx took the Ricardian model of the price of capital and the principle of scarcity as the basis of a more thorough analysis of the dynamics of capitalism in a world where capital was primarily industrial (machinery, plants, etc.) rather than landed property, so that in principle there was no limit to the amount of capital that could be accumulated. In fact, his principal conclusion was what one might call the "principle of infinite accumulation," that is, the inexorable tendency for capital to accumulate and become concentrated in ever fewer hands, with no natural limit to the process. This is the basis of Marx's prediction of an apocalyptic end to capitalism: either the rate of return on capital would steadily diminish (thereby killing the engine of accumulation and leading to violent conflict among 6 7 capitalists), or capital's share of national income would increase indefinitely (which sooner or later would unite the workers in revolt). In either case, no stable socioeconomic or political equilibriumwas possible. Marx's dark prophecy came no closer to being realized than Ricardo's. In the last third of the nineteenth century, wages finally began to increase: the improvement in the purchasing power of workers spread everywhere, and this changed the situation radically, even if extreme inequalities persisted and in some respects continued to increase until World War I. The communist revolution did indeed take place, but in the most backward country in Europe, Russia, where the Industrial Revolution had scarcely begun, whereas the most advanced European countries explored other, social democratic avenues—fortunately for their citizens. Like his predecessors, Marx totally neglected the possibility of durable technological progress and steadily increasing productivity, which is a force that can to some extent serve as a counterweight to the process of accumulation and concentration of private capital. He no doubt lacked the statistical data needed to refine his predictions. He probably suffered as well from having decided on his conclusions in 1848, before embarking on the research needed to justify them. Marx evidently wrote in great political fervor, which at times led him to issue hasty pronouncements from which it was difficult to escape. That is why economic theory needs to be rooted in historical sources that are as complete as possible, and in this respect Marx did not exploit all the possibilities available to him. What is more, he devoted little thought to the question of how a society in which private capital had been totally abolished would be organized politically and economically—a complex issue if ever there was one, as shown by the tragic totalitarian experiments undertaken in states where private capital was abolished. Despite these limitations, Marx's analysis remains relevant in several respects. First, he began with an important question (concerning the unprecedented concentration of wealth during the Industrial Revolution) and tried to answer it with the means at his disposal: economists today would do well to take inspiration from his example. Even more important, the principle of infinite accumulation that Marx proposed contains a key insight, as valid for the study of the twenty-first century as it was for the nineteenth and in some respects more worrisome than Ricardo's principle of scarcity. If the rates of population and productivity growth are relatively low, then accumulated wealth naturally takes on considerable importance, especially if it grows to extreme proportions and becomes socially destabilizing. In other words, low growth cannot adequately counterbalance the Marxist principle of infinite accumulation: the resulting equilibrium is not as apocalyptic as the one predicted by Marx but is nevertheless quite disturbing. Accumulation ends at a finite level, but that level may be high enough to be destabilizing. In particular, the very high level of private wealth that has been attained since the 1980s and 1990s in the wealthy countries of Europe and in Japan, measured in years of national income, directly reflects the Marxian logic. From Marx to Kuznets, or Apocalypse to Fairy Tale Turning from the nineteenth-century analyses of Ricardo and Marx to the twentieth-century analyses of Simon Kuznets, we might say that economists' no doubt overly developed taste for apocalyptic predictions gave way to a similarly excessive fondness for fairy tales, or at any rate happy endings.

According to Kuznets's theory, income inequality would automatically decrease in advanced phases 8 of capitalist development, regardless of economic policy choices or other differences between countries, until eventually it stabilized at an acceptable level. Proposed in 1955, this was really a theory of the magical postwar years referred to in France as the "Trente Glorieuses," the thirty glorious years from 1945 to 1975. For Kuznets, it was enough to be patient, and before long growth would benefit everyone. The philosophy of the moment was summed up in a single sentence: "Growth is a rising tide that lifts all boats." A similar optimism can also be seen in Robert Solow's 1956 analysis of the conditions necessary for an economy to achieve a "balanced growth path," that is, a growth trajectory along which all variables—output, incomes, profits, wages, capital, asset prices, and so on—would progress at the same pace, so that every social group would benefit from growth to the same degree, with no major deviations from the norm. Kuznets's position was thus diametrically opposed to the Ricardian and Marxist idea of an inegalitarian spiral and antithetical to the apocalyptic predictions of the nineteenth century. In order to properly convey the considerable influence that Kuznets's theory enjoyed in the 1980s and 1990s and to a certain extent still enjoys today, it is important to emphasize that it was the first theory of this sort to rely on a formidable statistical apparatus. It was not until the middle of the twentieth century, in fact, that the first historical series of income distribution statistics became available with the publication in 1953 of Kuznets's monumental Shares of Upper Income Groups in Income and Savings. Kuznets's series dealt with only one country (the United States) over a period of thirty-five years (1913–1948). It was nevertheless a major contribution, which drew on two sources of data totally unavailable to nineteenth-century authors: US federal income tax returns (which did not exist before the creation of the income tax in 1913) and Kuznets's own estimates of US national income from a few years earlier. This was the very first attempt to measure social inequality on such an ambitious scale. It is important to realize that without these two complementary and indispensable datasets, it is simply impossible to measure inequality in the income distribution or to gauge its evolution over time. To be sure, the first attempts to estimate national income in Britain and France date back to the late seventeenth and early eighteenth century, and there would be many more such attempts over the course of the nineteenth century. But these were isolated estimates. It was not until the twentieth century, in the years between the two world wars, that the first yearly series of national income data were developed by economists such as Kuznets and John W. Kendrick in the United States, Arthur Bowley and Colin Clark in Britain, and L. Dugé de Bernonville in France. This type of data allows us to measure a country's total income. In order to gauge the share of high incomes in national income, we also need statements of income. Such information became available when many countries adopted a progressive income tax around the time of World War I (1913 in the United States, 1914 in France, 1909 in Britain, 1922 in India, 1932 in Argentina). It is crucial to recognize that even where there is no income tax, there are still all sorts of statistics concerning whatever tax basis exists at a given point in time (for example, the distribution of the number of doors and windows by département in nineteenth-century France, which is not without interest), but these data tell us nothing about incomes. What is more, before the requirement to declare one's income to the tax authorities was enacted in law, people were often unaware of the amount of their own income. The same is true of the corporate tax and wealth tax. Taxation is not only a way of 9 10 11 12 requiring all citizens to contribute to the financing of public expenditures and projects and to distribute the tax burden as fairly as possible; it is also useful for establishing classifications and promoting knowledge as well as democratic transparency. In any event, the data that Kuznets collected allowed him to calculate the evolution of the share of each decile, as well as of the upper centiles, of the income hierarchy in total US national income. What did he find? He noted a sharp reduction in income inequality in the United States between 1913 and 1948. More specifically, at the beginning of this period, the upper decile of the income distribution (that is, the top 10 percent of US earners) claimed 45–50 percent of annual national income. By the late 1940s, the share of the top decile had decreased to roughly 30–35 percent of national income. This decrease of nearly 10 percentage points was considerable: for example, it was equal to half the income of the poorest 50 percent of Americans. The reduction of inequality was clear and incontrovertible. This was news of considerable importance, and it had an enormous impact on economic debate in the postwar era in both universities and international organizations. Malthus, Ricardo, Marx, and many others had been talking about inequalities for decades without citing any sources whatsoever or any methods for comparing one era with another or deciding between competing hypotheses. Now, for the first time, objective data were available. Although the information was not perfect, it had the merit of existing. What is more, the work of compilation was extremely well documented: the weighty volume that Kuznets published in 1953 revealed his sources and methods in the most minute detail, so that every calculation could be reproduced. And besides that, Kuznets was the bearer of good news: inequality was shrinking. The Kuznets Curve: Good News in the Midst of the Cold War In fact, Kuznets himself was well aware that the compression of high US incomes between 1913 and 1948 was largely accidental. It stemmed in large part from multiple shocks triggered by the Great Depression and World War II and had little to do with any natural or automatic process. In his 1953 work, he analyzed his series in detail and warned readers not to make hasty generalizations. But in December 1954, at the Detroit meeting of the American Economic Association, of which he was president, he offered a far more optimistic interpretation of his results than he had given in 1953. It was this lecture, published in 1955 under the title "Economic Growth and Income Inequality," that gave rise to the theory of the "Kuznets curve." According to this theory, inequality everywhere can be expected to follow a "bell curve." In other words, it should first increase and then decrease over the course of industrialization and economic development. According to Kuznets, a first phase of naturally increasing inequality associated with the early stages of industrialization, which in the United States meant, broadly speaking, the nineteenth century, would be followed by a phase of sharply decreasing inequality, which in the United States allegedly began in the first half of the twentieth century. Kuznets's 1955 paper is enlightening. After reminding readers of all the reasons for interpreting the data cautiously and noting the obvious importance of exogenous shocks in the recent reduction of inequality in the United States, Kuznets suggests, almost innocently in passing, that the internal logic of economic development might also yield the same result, quite apart from any policy intervention or external shock. The idea was that inequalities increase in the early phases of industrialization, 13 because only a minority is prepared to benefit from the new wealth that industrialization brings. Later, in more advanced phases of development, inequality automatically decreases as a larger and larger fraction of the population partakes of the fruits of economic growth. The "advanced phase" of industrial development is supposed to have begun toward the end of the nineteenth or the beginning of the twentieth century in the industrialized countries, and the reduction of inequality observed in the United States between 1913 and 1948 could therefore be portrayed as one instance of a more general phenomenon, which should theoretically reproduce itself everywhere, including underdeveloped countries then mired in postcolonial poverty. The data Kuznets had presented in his 1953 book suddenly became a powerful political weapon. He was well aware of the highly speculative nature of his theorizing. Nevertheless, by presenting such an optimistic theory in the context of a "presidential address" to the main professional association of US economists, an audience that was inclined to believe and disseminate the good news delivered by their prestigious leader, he knew that he would wield considerable influence: thus the "Kuznets curve" was born. In order to make sure that everyone understood what was at stake, he took care to remind his listeners that the intent of his optimistic predictions was quite simply to maintain the underdeveloped countries "within the orbit of the free world." In large part, then, the theory of the Kuznets curve was a product of the Cold War. To avoid any misunderstanding, let me say that Kuznets's work in establishing the first US national accounts data and the first historical series of inequality measures was of the utmost importance, and it is clear from reading his books (as opposed to his papers) that he shared the true scientific ethic. In addition, the high growth rates observed in all the developed countries in the post–World War II period were a phenomenon of great significance, as was the still more significant fact that all social groups shared in the fruits of growth. It is quite understandable that the Trente Glorieuses fostered a certain degree of optimism and that the apocalyptic predictions of the nineteenth century concerning the distribution of wealth forfeited some of their popularity. Nevertheless, the magical Kuznets curve theory was formulated in large part for the wrong reasons, and its empirical underpinnings were extremely fragile. The sharp reduction in income inequality that we observe in almost all the rich countries between 1914 and 1945 was due above all to the world wars and the violent economic and political shocks they entailed (especially for people with large fortunes). It had little to do with the tranquil process of intersectoral mobility described by Kuznets. Putting the Distributional Question Back at the Heart of Economic Analysis The question is important, and not just for historical reasons. Since the 1970s, income inequality has increased significantly in the rich countries, especially the United States, where the concentration of income in the first decade of the twenty-first century regained—indeed, slightly exceeded—the level attained in the second decade of the previous century. It is therefore crucial to understand clearly why and how inequality decreased in the interim. To be sure, the very rapid growth of poor and emerging countries, especially China, may well prove to be a potent force for reducing inequalities at the global level, just as the growth of the rich countries did during the period 1945–1975. But this process has generated deep anxiety in the emerging countries and even deeper anxiety in the rich countries. Furthermore, the impressive disequilibria observed in recent decades in the financial, oil, 14 15 16 17 and real estate markets have naturally aroused doubts as to the inevitability of the "balanced growth path" described by Solow and Kuznets, according to whom all key economic variables are supposed to move at the same pace. Will the world in 2050 or 2100 be owned by traders, top managers, and the superrich, or will it belong to the oil-producing countries or the Bank of China? Or perhaps it will be owned by the tax havens in which many of these actors will have sought refuge. It would be absurd not to raise the question of who will own what and simply to assume from the outset that growth is naturally "balanced" in the long run. In a way, we are in the same position at the beginning of the twenty-first century as our forebears were in the early nineteenth century: we are witnessing impressive changes in economies around the world, and it is very difficult to know how extensive they will turn out to be or what the global distribution of wealth, both within and between countries, will look like several decades from now. The economists of the nineteenth century deserve immense credit for placing the distributional question at the heart of economic analysis and for seeking to study long-term trends. Their answers were not always satisfactory, but at least they were asking the right questions. There is no fundamental reason why we should believe that growth is automatically balanced. It is long since past the time when we should have put the question of inequality back at the center of economic analysis and begun asking questions first raised in the nineteenth century. For far too long, economists have neglected the distribution of wealth, partly because of Kuznets's optimistic conclusions and partly because of the profession's undue enthusiasm for simplistic mathematical models based on so-called representative agents. If the question of inequality is again to become central, we must begin by gathering as extensive as possible a set of historical data for the purpose of understanding past and present trends. For it is by patiently establishing facts and patterns and then comparing different countries that we can hope to identify the mechanisms at work and gain a clearer idea of the future.

Contents

CHAPTER ONE

Income and Output

On August 16, 2012, the South African police intervened in a labor conflict between workers at the Marikana platinum mine near Johannesburg and the mine's owners: the stockholders of Lonmin, Inc., based in London. Police fired on the strikers with live ammunition. Thirty-four miners were killed. As often in such strikes, the conflict primarily concerned wages: the miners had asked for a doubling of their wage from 500 to 1,000 euros a month. After the tragic loss of life, the company finally proposed a monthly raise of 75 euros. This episode reminds us, if we needed reminding, that the question of what share of output should go to wages and what share to profits—in other words, how should the income from production be divided between labor and capital?—has always been at the heart of distributional conflict. In traditional societies, the basis of social inequality and most common cause of rebellion was the conflict of interest between landlord and peasant, between those who owned land and those who cultivated it with their labor, those who received land rents and those who paid them. The Industrial Revolution exacerbated the conflict between capital and labor, perhaps because production became more capital intensive than in the past (making use of machinery and exploiting natural resources more than ever before) and perhaps, too, because hopes for a more equitable distribution of income and a more democratic social order were dashed. I will come back to this point. The Marikana tragedy calls to mind earlier instances of violence. At Haymarket Square in Chicago on May 1, 1886, and then at Fourmies, in northern France, on May 1, 1891, police fired on workers striking for higher wages. Does this kind of violent clash between labor and capital belong to the past, or will it be an integral part of twenty-first-century history? The first two parts of this book focus on the respective shares of global income going to labor and capital and on how those shares have changed since the eighteenth century. I will temporarily set aside the issue of income inequality between workers (for example, between an ordinary worker, an engineer, and a plant manager) and between capitalists (for example, between small, medium, and large stockholders or landlords) until Part Three. Clearly, each of these two dimensions of the distribution of wealth—the "factorial" distribution in which labor and capital are treated as "factors of production," viewed in the abstract as homogeneous entities, and the "individual" distribution, which takes account of inequalities of income from labor and capital at the individual level—is in practice fundamentally important. It is impossible to achieve a satisfactory understanding of the distributional problem without analyzing both. In any case, the Marikana miners were striking not only against what they took to be Lonmin's excessive profits but also against the apparently fabulous salary awarded to the mine's manager and the difference between his compensation and theirs. Indeed, if capital ownership were equally distributed and each worker received an equal share of profits in addition to his or her wages, virtually no one would be interested in the division of earnings between profits and wages. If the capital-labor split gives rise to so many conflicts, it is due first and foremost to the extreme 1 2 3 4 concentration of the ownership of capital. Inequality of wealth—and of the consequent income fromcapital—is in fact always much greater than inequality of income from labor. I will analyze this phenomenon and its causes in Part Three. For now, I will take the inequality of income from labor and capital as given and focus on the global division of national income between capital and labor. To be clear, my purpose here is not to plead the case of workers against owners but rather to gain as clear as possible a view of reality. Symbolically, the inequality of capital and labor is an issue that arouses strong emotions. It clashes with widely held ideas of what is and is not just, and it is hardly surprising if this sometimes leads to physical violence. For those who own nothing but their labor power and who often live in humble conditions (not to say wretched conditions in the case of eighteenth-century peasants or the Marikana miners), it is difficult to accept that the owners of capital —some of whom have inherited at least part of their wealth—are able to appropriate so much of the wealth produced by their labor. Capital's share can be quite large: often as much as one-quarter of total output and sometimes as high as one-half in capital-intensive sectors such as mining, or even more where local monopolies allow the owners of capital to demand an even larger share. Of course, everyone can also understand that if all the company's earnings from its output went to paying wages and nothing to profits, it would probably be difficult to attract the capital needed to finance new investments, at least as our economies are currently organized (to be sure, one can imagine other forms of organization). Furthermore, it is not necessarily just to deny any remuneration to those who choose to save more than others—assuming, of course, that differences in saving are an important reason for the inequality of wealth. Bear in mind, too, that a portion of what is called "the income of capital" may be remuneration for "entrepreneurial" labor, and this should no doubt be treated as we treat other forms of labor. This classic argument deserves closer scrutiny. Taking all these elements into account, what is the "right" split between capital and labor? Can we be sure that an economy based on the "free market" and private property always and everywhere leads to an optimal division, as if by magic? In an ideal society, how would one arrange the division between capital and labor? How should one think about the problem? The Capital-Labor Split in the Long Run: Not So Stable If this study is to make even modest progress on these questions and at least clarify the terms of a debate that appears to be endless, it will be useful to begin by establishing some facts as accurately and carefully as possible. What exactly do we know about the evolution of the capital-labor split since the eighteenth century? For a long time, the idea accepted by most economists and uncritically repeated in textbooks was that the relative shares of labor and capital in national income were quite stable over the long run, with the generally accepted figure being two-thirds for labor and one-third for capital. Today, with the advantage of greater historical perspective and newly available data, it is clear that the reality was quite a bit more complex. For one thing, the capital-labor split varied widely over the course of the twentieth century. The changes observed in the nineteenth century, which I touched on in the Introduction (an increase in the capital share in the first half of the century, followed by a slight decrease and then a period of stability), seem mild by comparison. Briefly, the shocks that buffeted the economy in the period 1914–1945—World War I, the Bolshevik Revolution of 1917, the Great Depression, World War II, 5 and the consequent advent of new regulatory and tax policies along with controls on capital—reduced capital's share of income to historically low levels in the 1950s. Very soon, however, capital began to reconstitute itself. The growth of capital's share accelerated with the victories of Margaret Thatcher in England in 1979 and Ronald Reagan in the United States in 1980, marking the beginning of a conservative revolution. Then came the collapse of the Soviet bloc in 1989, followed by financial globalization and deregulation in the 1990s. All of these events marked a political turn in the opposite direction from that observed in the first half of the twentieth century. By 2010, and despite the crisis that began in 2007–2008, capital was prospering as it had not done since 1913. Not all of the consequences of capital's renewed prosperity were negative; to some extent it was a natural and desirable development. But it has changed the way we look at the capital-labor split since the beginning of the twenty-first century, as well as our view of changes likely to occur in the decades to come. Furthermore, if we look beyond the twentieth century and adopt a very long-term view, the idea of a stable capital-labor split must somehow deal with the fact that the nature of capital itself has changed radically (from land and other real estate in the eighteenth century to industrial and financial capital in the twenty-first century). There is also the idea, widespread among economists, that modern economic growth depends largely on the rise of "human capital." At first glance, this would seem to imply that labor should claim a growing share of national income. And one does indeed find that there may be a tendency for labor's share to increase over the very long run, but the gains are relatively modest: capital's share (excluding human capital) in the early decades of the twenty-first century is only slightly smaller than it was at the beginning of the nineteenth century. The importance of capital in the wealthy countries today is primarily due to a slowing of both demographic growth and productivity growth, coupled with political regimes that objectively favor private capital. The most fruitful way to understand these changes is to analyze the evolution of the capital/income ratio (that is, the ratio of the total stock of capital to the annual flow of income) rather than focus exclusively on the capital-labor split (that is, the share of income going to capital and labor, respectively). In the past, scholars have mainly studied the latter, largely owing to the lack of adequate data to do anything else. Before presenting my results in detail, it is best to proceed by stages. The purpose of Part One of this book is to introduce certain basic notions. In the remainder of this chapter, I will begin by presenting the concepts of domestic product and national income, capital and labor, and the capital/income ratio. Then I will look at how the global distribution of income has changed since the Industrial Revolution. In Chapter 2, I will analyze the general evolution of growth rates over time. This will play a central role in the subsequent analysis. With these preliminaries out of the way, Part Two takes up the dynamics of the capital/income ratio and the capital-labor split, once again proceeding by stages. Chapter 3 will look at changes in the composition of capital and the capital/income ratio since the eighteenth century, beginning with Britain and France, about which we have the best long-run data. Chapter 4 introduces the German case and above all looks at the United States, which serves as a useful complement to the European prism. Finally, Chapters 5 and 6 attempt to extend the analysis to all the rich countries of the world and, insofar as possible, to the entire planet. I also attempt to draw conclusions relevant to the global dynamics of the capital/income ratio and capital-labor split in the twenty-first century. The Idea of National Income It will be useful to begin with the concept of "national income," to which I will frequently refer in what follows. National income is defined as the sum of all income available to the residents of a given country in a given year, regardless of the legal classification of that income. National income is closely related to the idea of GDP, which comes up often in public debate. There are, however, two important differences between GDP and national income. GDP measures the total of goods and services produced in a given year within the borders of a given country. In order to calculate national income, one must first subtract from GDP the depreciation of the capital that made this production possible: in other words, one must deduct wear and tear on buildings, infrastructure, machinery, vehicles, computers, and other items during the year in question. This depreciation is substantial, today on the order of 10 percent of GDP in most countries, and it does not correspond to anyone's income: before wages are distributed to workers or dividends to stockholders, and before genuinely new investments are made, worn-out capital must be replaced or repaired. If this is not done, wealth is lost, resulting in negative income for the owners. When depreciation is subtracted from GDP, one obtains the "net domestic product," which I will refer to more simply as "domestic output" or "domestic production," which is typically 90 percent of GDP. Then one must add net income received from abroad (or subtract net income paid to foreigners, depending on each country's situation). For example, a country whose firms and other capital assets are owned by foreigners may well have a high domestic product but a much lower national income, once profits and rents flowing abroad are deducted from the total. Conversely, a country that owns a large portion of the capital of other countries may enjoy a national income much higher than its domestic product. Later I will give examples of both of these situations, drawn from the history of capitalism as well as from today's world. I should say at once that this type of international inequality can give rise to great political tension. It is not an insignificant thing when one country works for another and pays out a substantial share of its output as dividends and rent to foreigners over a long period of time. In many cases, such a system can survive (to a point) only if sustained by relations of political domination, as was the case in the colonial era, when Europe effectively owned much of the rest of the world. A key question of this research is the following: Under what conditions is this type of situation likely to recur in the twenty-first century, possibly in some novel geographic configuration? For example, Europe, rather than being the owner, may find itself owned. Such fears are currently widespread in the Old World—perhaps too widespread. We shall see. At this stage, suffice it to say that most countries, whether wealthy or emergent, are currently in much more balanced situations than one sometimes imagines. In France as in the United States, Germany as well as Great Britain, China as well as Brazil, and Japan as well as Italy, national income is within 1 or 2 percent of domestic product. In all these countries, in other words, the inflow of profits, interest, dividends, rent, and so on is more or less balanced by a comparable outflow. In wealthy countries, net income from abroad is generally slightly positive. To a first approximation, the residents of these countries own as much in foreign real estate and financial instruments as foreigners own of theirs. Contrary to a tenacious myth, France is not owned by California pension funds or the Bank of China, any more than the United States belongs to Japanese and German investors. The fear of getting into such a predicament is so strong today that fantasy often outstrips reality. The reality is that inequality with respect to capital is a far greater domestic issue than it is an international one. Inequality in the ownership of capital brings the rich and poor within each country into conflict with one another far more than it pits one country against another. This has not always been the case, however, and it is perfectly legitimate to ask whether our future may not look more like our past, particularly since certain countries—Japan, Germany, the oil-exporting countries, and to a lesser degree China—have in recent years accumulated substantial claims on the rest of the world (though by no means as large as the record claims of the colonial era). Furthermore, the very substantial increase in cross-ownership, in which various countries own substantial shares of one another, can give rise to a legitimate sense of dispossession, even when net asset positions are close to zero. To sum up, a country's national income may be greater or smaller than its domestic product, depending on whether net income from abroad is positive or negative. National income = domestic output + net income from abroad At the global level, income received from abroad and paid abroad must balance, so that income is by definition equal to output: Global income = global output This equality between two annual flows, income and output, is an accounting identity, yet it reflects an important reality. In any given year, it is impossible for total income to exceed the amount of new wealth that is produced (globally speaking; a single country may of course borrow from abroad). Conversely, all production must be distributed as income in one form or another, to either labor or capital: whether as wages, salaries, honoraria, bonuses, and so on (that is, as payments to workers and others who contributed labor to the process of production) or else as profits, dividends, interest, rents, royalties, and so on (that is, as payments to the owners of capital used in the process of production). What Is Capital? To recapitulate: regardless of whether we are looking at the accounts of a company, a nation, or the global economy, the associated output and income can be decomposed as the sum of income to capital and income to labor: National income = capital income + labor income But what is capital? What are its limits? What forms does it take? How has its composition changed over time? This question, central to this investigation, will be examined in greater detail in 6 7 subsequent chapters. For now it will suffice to make the following points: First, throughout this book, when I speak of "capital" without further qualification, I always exclude what economists often call (unfortunately, to my mind) "human capital," which consists of an individual's labor power, skills, training, and abilities. In this book, capital is defined as the sumtotal of nonhuman assets that can be owned and exchanged on some market. Capital includes all forms of real property (including residential real estate) as well as financial and professional capital (plants, infrastructure, machinery, patents, and so on) used by firms and government agencies. There are many reasons for excluding human capital from our definition of capital. The most obvious is that human capital cannot be owned by another person or traded on a market (not permanently, at any rate). This is a key difference from other forms of capital. One can of course put one's labor services up for hire under a labor contract of some sort. In all modern legal systems, however, such an arrangement has to be limited in both time and scope. In slave societies, of course, this is obviously not true: there, a slaveholder can fully and completely own the human capital of another person and even of that person's offspring. In such societies, slaves can be bought and sold on the market and conveyed by inheritance, and it is common to include slaves in calculating a slaveholder's wealth. I will show how this worked when I examine the composition of private capital in the southern United States before 1865. Leaving such special (and for now historical) cases aside, it makes little sense to attempt to add human and nonhuman capital. Throughout history, both forms of wealth have played fundamental and complementary roles in economic growth and development and will continue to do so in the twenty-first century. But in order to understand the growth process and the inequalities it engenders, we must distinguish carefully between human and nonhuman capital and treat each one separately. Nonhuman capital, which in this book I will call simply "capital," includes all forms of wealth that individuals (or groups of individuals) can own and that can be transferred or traded through the market on a permanent basis. In practice, capital can be owned by private individuals (in which case we speak of "private capital") or by the government or government agencies (in which case we speak of "public capital"). There are also intermediate forms of collective property owned by "moral persons" (that is, entities such as foundations and churches) pursuing specific aims. I will come back to this. The boundary between what private individuals can and cannot own has evolved considerably over time and around the world, as the extreme case of slavery indicates. The same is true of property in the atmosphere, the sea, mountains, historical monuments, and knowledge. Certain private interests would like to own these things, and sometimes they justify this desire on grounds of efficiency rather than mere self-interest. But there is no guarantee that this desire coincides with the general interest. Capital is not an immutable concept: it reflects the state of development and prevailing social relations of each society. Capital and Wealth To simplify the text, I use the words "capital" and "wealth" interchangeably, as if they were perfectly synonymous. By some definitions, it would be better to reserve the word "capital" to describe forms of wealth accumulated by human beings (buildings, machinery, infrastructure, etc.) and therefore to exclude land and natural resources, with which humans have been endowed without having to accumulate them. Land would then be a component of wealth but not of capital. The problem is that it is not always easy to distinguish the value of buildings from the value of the land on which they are built. An even greater difficulty is that it is very hard to gauge the value of "virgin" land (as humans found it centuries or millennia ago) apart from improvements due to human intervention, such as drainage, irrigation, fertilization, and so on. The same problem arises in connection with natural resources such as petroleum, gas, rare earth elements, and the like, whose pure value is hard to distinguish from the value added by the investments needed to discover new deposits and prepare them for exploitation. I therefore include all these forms of wealth in capital. Of course, this choice does not eliminate the need to look closely at the origins of wealth, especially the boundary line between accumulation and appropriation. Some definitions of "capital" hold that the term should apply only to those components of wealth directly employed in the production process. For instance, gold might be counted as part of wealth but not of capital, because gold is said to be useful only as a store of value. Once again, this limitation strikes me as neither desirable nor practical (because gold can be a factor of production, not only in the manufacture of jewelry but also in electronics and nanotechnology). Capital in all its forms has always played a dual role, as both a store of value and a factor of production. I therefore decided that it was simpler not to impose a rigid distinction between wealth and capital. Similarly, I ruled out the idea of excluding residential real estate from capital on the grounds that it is "unproductive," unlike the "productive capital" used by firms and government: industrial plants, office buildings, machinery, infrastructure, and so on. The truth is that all these forms of wealth are useful and productive and reflect capital's two major economic functions. Residential real estate can be seen as a capital asset that yields "housing services," whose value is measured by their rental equivalent. Other capital assets can serve as factors of production for firms and government agencies that produce goods and services (and need plants, offices, machinery, infrastructure, etc. to do so). Each of these two types of capital currently accounts for roughly half the capital stock in the developed countries. To summarize, I define "national wealth" or "national capital" as the total market value of everything owned by the residents and government of a given country at a given point in time, provided that it can be traded on some market. It consists of the sum total of nonfinancial assets (land, dwellings, commercial inventory, other buildings, machinery, infrastructure, patents, and other directly owned professional assets) and financial assets (bank accounts, mutual funds, bonds, stocks, financial investments of all kinds, insurance policies, pension funds, etc.), less the total amount of financial liabilities (debt). If we look only at the assets and liabilities of private individuals, the result is private wealth or private capital. If we consider assets and liabilities held by the government and other governmental entities (such as towns, social insurance agencies, etc.), the result is public wealth or public capital. By definition, national wealth is the sum of these two terms: National wealth = private wealth + public wealth Public wealth in most developed countries is currently insignificant (or even negative, where the public debt exceeds public assets). As I will show, private wealth accounts for nearly all of national 8 9 wealth almost everywhere. This has not always been the case, however, so it is important to distinguish clearly between the two notions. To be clear, although my concept of capital excludes human capital (which cannot be exchanged on any market in nonslave societies), it is not limited to "physical" capital (land, buildings, infrastructure, and other material goods). I include "immaterial" capital such as patents and other intellectual property, which are counted either as nonfinancial assets (if individuals hold patents directly) or as financial assets (when an individual owns shares of a corporation that holds patents, as is more commonly the case). More broadly, many forms of immaterial capital are taken into account by way of the stock market capitalization of corporations. For instance, the stock market value of a company often depends on its reputation and trademarks, its information systems and modes of organization, its investments, whether material or immaterial, for the purpose of making its products and services more visible and attractive, and so on. All of this is reflected in the price of common stock and other corporate financial assets and therefore in national wealth. To be sure, the price that the financial markets sets on a company's or even a sector's immaterial capital at any given moment is largely arbitrary and uncertain. We see this in the collapse of the Internet bubble in 2000, in the financial crisis that began in 2007–2008, and more generally in the enormous volatility of the stock market. The important fact to note for now is that this is a characteristic of all forms of capital, not just immaterial capital. Whether we are speaking of a building or a company, a manufacturing firm or a service firm, it is always very difficult to set a price on capital. Yet as I will show, total national wealth, that is, the wealth of a country as a whole and not of any particular type of asset, obeys certain laws and conforms to certain regular patterns. One further point: total national wealth can always be broken down into domestic capital and foreign capital: National wealth = national capital = domestic capital + net foreign capital Domestic capital is the value of the capital stock (buildings, firms, etc.) located within the borders of the country in question. Net foreign capital—or net foreign assets—measures the country's position vis-à-vis the rest of the world: more specifically, it is the difference between assets owned by the country's citizens in the rest of the world and assets of the country owned by citizens of other countries. On the eve of World War I, Britain and France both enjoyed significant net positive asset positions vis-à-vis the rest of the world. One characteristic of the financial globalization that has taken place since the 1980s is that many countries have more or less balanced net asset positions, but those positions are quite large in absolute terms. In other words, many countries have large capital stakes in other countries, but those other countries also have stakes in the country in question, and the two positions are more or less equal, so that net foreign capital is close to zero. Globally, of course, all the net positions must add up to zero, so that total global wealth equals the "domestic" capital of the planet as a whole. The Capital/Income Ratio Now that income and capital have been defined, I can move on to the first basic law tying these two ideas together. I begin by defining the capital/income ratio. Income is a flow. It corresponds to the quantity of goods produced and distributed in a given period (which we generally take to be a year). Capital is a stock. It corresponds to the total wealth owned at a given point in time. This stock comes from the wealth appropriated or accumulated in all prior years combined. The most natural and useful way to measure the capital stock in a particular country is to divide that stock by the annual flow of income. This gives us the capital/income ratio, which I denote by the Greek letter β. For example, if a country's total capital stock is the equivalent of six years of national income, we write $\beta = 6$ (or $\beta = 600\%$). In the developed countries today, the capital/income ratio generally varies between 5 and 6, and the capital stock consists almost entirely of private capital. In France and Britain, Germany and Italy, the United States and Japan, national income was roughly 30,000–35,000 euros per capita in 2010, whereas total private wealth (net of debt) was typically on the order of 150,000–200,000 euros per capita, or five to six times annual national income. There are interesting variations both within Europe and around the world. For instance, β is greater than 6 in Japan and Italy and less than 5 in the United States and Germany. Public wealth is just barely positive in some countries and slightly negative in others. And so on. I examine all this in detail in the next few chapters. At this point, it is enough to keep these orders of magnitude in mind, in order to make the ideas as concrete as possible. The fact that national income in the wealthy countries of the world in 2010 was on the order of 30,000 euros per capita per annum (or 2,500 euros per month) obviously does not mean that everyone earns that amount. Like all averages, this average income figure hides enormous disparities. In practice, many people earn much less than 2,500 euros a month, while others earn dozens of times that much. Income disparities are partly the result of unequal pay for work and partly of much larger inequalities in income from capital, which are themselves a consequence of the extreme concentration of wealth. The average national income per capita is simply the amount that one could distribute to each individual if it were possible to equalize the income distribution without altering total output or national income. Similarly, private per capita wealth on the order of 180,000 euros, or six years of national income, does not mean that everyone owns that much capital. Many people have much less, while some own millions or tens of millions of euros' worth of capital assets. Much of the population has very little accumulated wealth—significantly less than one year's income: a few thousand euros in a bank account, the equivalent of a few weeks' or months' worth of wages. Some people even have negative wealth: in other words, the goods they own are worth less than the debts they owe. By contrast, others have considerable fortunes, ranging from ten to twenty times their annual income or even more. The capital/income ratio for the country as a whole tells us nothing about inequalities within the country. But β does measure the overall importance of capital in a society, so analyzing this ratio is a necessary first step in the study of inequality. The main purpose of Part Two is to understand how and why the capital/income ratio varies from country to country, and how it has evolved over time. To appreciate the concrete form that wealth takes in today's world, it is useful to note that the 10 11 capital stock in the developed countries currently consists of two roughly equal shares: residential capital and professional capital used by firms and government. To sum up, each citizen of one of the wealthy countries earned an average of 30,000 euros per year in 2010, owned approximately 180,000 euros of capital, 90,000 in the form of a dwelling and another 90,000 in stocks, bonds, savings, or other investments. There are interesting variations across countries, which I will analyze in Chapter 2. For now, the fact that capital can be divided into two roughly equal shares will be useful to keep in mind. The First Fundamental Law of Capitalism: $\alpha = r \times \beta$ I can now present the first fundamental law of capitalism, which links the capital stock to the flow of income from capital. The capital/income ratio β is related in a simple way to the share of income from capital in national income, denoted α. The formula is $\alpha = r \times \beta$ where r is the rate of return on capital. For example, if $\beta = 600\%$ and $r = 5\%$, then $\alpha = r \times \beta = 30\%$. In other words, if national wealth represents the equivalent of six years of national income, and if the rate of return on capital is 5 percent per year, then capital's share in national income is 30 percent. The formula $\alpha = r \times \beta$ is a pure accounting identity. It can be applied to all societies in all periods of history, by definition. Though tautological, it should nevertheless be regarded as the first fundamental law of capitalism, because it expresses a simple, transparent relationship among the three most important concepts for analyzing the capitalist system: the capital/income ratio, the share of capital in income, and the rate of return on capital. The rate of return on capital is a central concept in many economic theories. In particular, Marxist analysis emphasizes the falling rate of profit—a historical prediction that turned out to be quite wrong, although it does contain an interesting intuition. The concept of the rate of return on capital also plays a central role in many other theories. In any case, the rate of return on capital measures the yield on capital over the course of a year regardless of its legal form (profits, rents, dividends, interest, royalties, capital gains, etc.), expressed as a percentage of the value of capital invested. It is therefore a broader notion than the "rate of profit," and much broader than the "rate of interest," while incorporating both. Obviously, the rate of return can vary widely, depending on the type of investment. Some firms generate rates of return greater than 10 percent per year; others make losses (negative rate of return). The average long-run rate of return on stocks is 7–8 percent in many countries. Investments in real estate and bonds frequently return 3–4 percent, while the real rate of interest on public debt is sometimes much lower. The formula $\alpha = r \times \beta$ tells us nothing about these subtleties, but it does tell us how to relate these three quantities, which can be useful for framing discussion. For example, in the wealthy countries around 2010, income from capital (profits, interests, dividends, rents, etc.) generally hovered around 30 percent of national income. With a capital/income 12 13 14 15 ratio on the order of 600 percent, this meant that the rate of return on capital was around 5 percent. Concretely, this means that the current per capita national income of 30,000 euros per year in rich countries breaks down as 21,000 euros per year income from labor (70 percent) and 9,000 euros income from capital (30 percent). Each citizen owns an average of 180,000 euros of capital, and the 9,000 euros of income from capital thus corresponds to an average annual return on capital of 5 percent. Once again, I am speaking here only of averages: some individuals receive far more than 9,000 euros per year in income from capital, while others receive nothing while paying rent to their landlords and interest to their creditors. Considerable country-to-country variation also exists. In addition, measuring the share of income from capital is often difficult in both a conceptual and a practical sense, because there are some categories of income (such as nonwage self-employment income and entrepreneurial income) that are hard to break down into income from capital and income from labor. In some cases this can make comparison misleading. When such problems arise, the least imperfect method of measuring the capital share of income may be to apply a plausible average rate of return to the capital/income ratio. At this stage, the orders of magnitude given above (β = 600%, α = 30%, r = 5%) may be taken as typical. For the sake of concreteness, let us note, too, that the average rate of return on land in rural societies is typically on the order of 4–5 percent. In the novels of Jane Austen and Honoré de Balzac, the fact that land (like government bonds) yields roughly 5 percent of the amount of capital invested (or, equivalently, that the value of capital corresponds to roughly twenty years of annual rent) is so taken for granted that it often goes unmentioned. Contemporary readers were well aware that it took capital on the order of 1 million francs to produce an annual rent of 50,000 francs. For nineteenthcentury novelists and their readers, the relation between capital and annual rent was self-evident, and the two measuring scales were used interchangeably, as if rent and capital were synonymous, or perfect equivalents in two different languages. Now, at the beginning of the twenty-first century, we find roughly the same return on real estate, 4– 5 percent, sometimes a little less, especially where prices have risen rapidly without dragging rents upward at the same rate. For example, in 2010, a large apartment in Paris, valued at 1 million euros, typically rents for slightly more than 2,500 euros per month, or annual rent of 30,000 euros, which corresponds to a return on capital of only 3 percent per year from the landlord's point of view. Such a rent is nevertheless quite high for a tenant living solely on income from labor (one hopes he or she is paid well) while it represents a significant income for the landlord. The bad news (or good news, depending on your point of view) is that things have always been like this. This type of rent tends to rise until the return on capital is around 4 percent (which in this example would correspond to a rent of 3,000–3,500 euros per month, or 40,000 per year). Hence this tenant's rent is likely to rise in the future. The landlord's annual return on investment may eventually be enhanced by a long-term capital gain on the value of the apartment. Smaller apartments yield a similar or perhaps slightly higher return. An apartment valued at 100,000 euros may yield 400 euros a month in rent, or nearly 5,000 per year (5 percent). A person who owns such an apartment and chooses to live in it can save the rental equivalent and devote that money to other uses, which yields a similar return on investment. Capital invested in businesses is of course at greater risk, so the average return is often higher. The stock-market capitalization of listed companies in various countries generally represents 12 to 15 years of annual profits, which corresponds to an annual return on investment of 6–8 percent (before taxes). The formula $\alpha = r \times \beta$ allows us to analyze the importance of capital for an entire country or even for the planet as a whole. It can also be used to study the accounts of a specific company. For example, take a firm that uses capital valued at 5 million euros (including offices, infrastructure, machinery, etc.) to produce 1 million euros worth of goods annually, with 600,000 euros going to pay workers and 400,000 euros in profits. The capital/income ratio of this company is $\beta = 5$ (its capital is equivalent to five years of output), the capital share α is 40 percent, and the rate of return on capital is $r = 8$ percent. Imagine another company that uses less capital (3 million euros) to produce the same output (1 million euros), but using more labor (700,000 euros in wages, 300,000 in profits). For this company, $\beta = 3$, $\alpha = 30$ percent, and $r = 10$ percent. The second firm is less capital intensive than the first, but it is more profitable (the rate of return on its capital is significantly higher). In all countries, the magnitudes of β, α, and r vary a great deal from company to company. Some sectors are more capital intensive than others: for example, the metal and energy sectors are more capital intensive than the textile and food processing sectors, and the manufacturing sector is more capital intensive than the service sector. There are also significant variations between firms in the same sector, depending on their choice of production technology and market position. The levels of β, α, and r in a given country also depend on the relative shares of residential real estate and natural resources in total capital. It bears emphasizing that the law $\alpha = r \times \beta$ does not tell us how each of these three variables is determined, or, in particular, how the national capital/income ratio (β) is determined, the latter being in some sense a measure of how intensely capitalistic the society in question is. To answer that question, we must introduce additional ideas and relationships, in particular the savings and investment rates and the rate of growth. This will lead us to the second fundamental law of capitalism: the higher the savings rate and the lower the growth rate, the higher the capital/income ratio (β). This will be shown in the next few chapters; at this stage, the law $\alpha = r \times \beta$ simply means that regardless of what economic, social, and political forces determine the level of the capital/income ratio (β), capital's share in income (α), and the rate of return on capital (r), these three variables are not independent of one another. Conceptually, there are two degrees of freedom, not three. National Accounts: An Evolving Social Construct Now that the key concepts of output and income, capital and wealth, capital/income ratio, and rate of return on capital have been explained, I will examine in greater detail how these abstract quantities can be measured and what such measurements can tell us about the historical evolution of the distribution of wealth in various countries. I will briefly review the main stages in the history of national accounts and then present a portrait in broad brushstrokes of how the global distribution of output and income has changed since the eighteenth century, along with a discussion of how demographic and economic growth rates have changed over the same period. These growth rates will 16 play an important part in the analysis. As noted, the first attempts to measure national income and capital date back to the late seventeenth and early eighteenth century. Around 1700, several isolated estimates appeared in Britain and France (apparently independently of one another). I am speaking primarily of the work of William Petty (1664) and Gregory King (1696) for England and Pierre le Pesant, sieur de Boisguillebert (1695), and Sébastien Le Prestre de Vauban (1707) for France. Their work focused on both the national stock of capital and the annual flow of national income. One of their primary objectives was to calculate the total value of land, by far the most important source of wealth in the agrarian societies of the day, and then to relate the quantity of landed wealth to the level of agricultural output and land rents. It is worth noting that these authors often had a political objective in mind, generally having to do with modernization of the tax system. By calculating the nation's income and wealth, they hoped to show the sovereign that it would be possible to raise tax receipts considerably while keeping tax rates relatively low, provided that all property and goods produced were subject to taxation and everyone was required to pay, including landlords of both aristocratic and common descent. This objective is obvious in Vauban's Projet de dîme royale (Plan for a Royal Tithe), but it is just as clear in the works of Boisguillebert and King (though less so in Petty's writing). The late eighteenth century saw further attempts to measure income and wealth, especially around the time of the French Revolution. Antoine Lavoisier published his estimates for the year 1789 in his book La Richesse territoriale du Royaume de France (The Territorial Wealth of the Kingdom of France), published in 1791. The new tax system established after the Revolution, which ended the privileges of the nobility and imposed a tax on all property in land, was largely inspired by this work, which was widely used to estimate expected receipts from new taxes. It was above all in the nineteenth century, however, that estimates of national wealth proliferated. From 1870 to 1900, Robert Giffen regularly updated his estimates of Britain's stock of national capital, which he compared to estimates by other authors (especially Patrick Colquhoun) from the early 1800s. Giffen marveled at the size of Britain's stock of industrial capital as well as the stock of foreign assets acquired since the Napoleonic wars, which was many times larger than the entire public debt due to those wars. In France at about the same time, Alfred de Foville and Clément Colson published estimates of "national wealth" and "private wealth," and, like Giffen, both writers also marveled at the considerable accumulation of private capital over the course of the nineteenth century. It was glaringly obvious to everyone that private fortunes were prospering in the period 1870–1914. For the economists of the day, the problem was to measure that wealth and compare different countries (the Franco-British rivalry was never far from their minds). Until World War I, estimates of wealth received much more attention than estimates of income and output, and there were in any case more of them, not only in Britain and France but also in Germany, the United States, and other industrial powers. In those days, being an economist meant first and foremost being able to estimate the national capital of one's country: this was almost a rite of initiation. It was not until the period between the two world wars that national accounts began to be established on an annual basis. Previous estimates had always focused on isolated years, with successive estimates separated by ten or more years, as in the case of Giffen's calculations of British national capital in the nineteenth century. In the 1930s, improvements in the primary statistical sources 17 made the first annual series of national income data possible. These generally went back as far as the beginning of the twentieth century or the last decades of the nineteenth. They were established for the United States by Kuznets and Kendrick, for Britain by Bowley and Clark, and for France by Dugé de Bernonville. After World War II, government statistical offices supplanted economists and began to compile and publish official annual data on GDP and national income. These official series continue to this day. Compared with the pre–World War I period, however, the focal point of the data had changed entirely. From the 1940s on, the primary motivation was to respond to the trauma of the Great Depression, during which governments had no reliable annual estimates of economic output. There was therefore a need for statistical and political tools in order to steer the economy properly and avoid a repeat of the catastrophe. Governments thus insisted on annual or even quarterly data on output and income. Estimates of national wealth, which had been so prized before 1914, now took a backseat, especially after the economic and political chaos of 1914–1945 made it difficult to interpret their meaning. Specifically, the prices of real estate and financial assets fell to extremely low levels, so low that private capital seemed to have evaporated. In the 1950s and 1960s, a period of reconstruction, the main goal was to measure the remarkable growth of output in various branches of industry. In the 1990s–2000s, wealth accounting again came to the fore. Economists and political leaders were well aware that the financial capitalism of the twenty-first century could not be properly analyzed with the tools of the 1950s and 1960s. In collaboration with central banks, government statistical agencies in various developed countries compiled and published annual series of data on the assets and liabilities of different groups, in addition to the usual income and output data. These wealth accounts are still far from perfect: for example, natural capital and damages to the environment are not well accounted for. Nevertheless, they represent real progress in comparison with national accounts from the early postwar years, which were concerned solely with endless growth in output. These are the official series that I use in this book to analyze aggregate wealth and the current capital/income ratio in the wealthy countries. One conclusion stands out in this brief history of national accounting: national accounts are a social construct in perpetual evolution. They always reflect the preoccupations of the era when they were conceived. We should be careful not to make a fetish of the published figures. When a country's national income per capita is said to be 30,000 euros, it is obvious that this number, like all economic and social statistics, should be regarded as an estimate, a construct, and not a mathematical certainty. It is simply the best estimate we have. National accounts represent the only consistent, systematic attempt to analyze a country's economic activity. They should be regarded as a limited and imperfect research tool, a compilation and arrangement of data from highly disparate sources. In all developed countries, national accounts are currently compiled by government statistical offices and central banks from the balance sheets and account books of financial and nonfinancial corporations together with many other statistical sources and surveys. We have no reason to think a priori that the officials involved in these efforts do not do their best to spot inconsistencies in the data in order to achieve the best possible estimates. Provided we use these data with caution and in a critical spirit and complement them with other data where there are errors or gaps (say, in dealing with tax havens), 18 19 these national accounts are an indispensable tool for estimating aggregate income and wealth. In particular, as I will show in Part Two, we can put together a consistent analysis of the historical evolution of the capital/income ratio by meticulously compiling and comparing national wealth estimates by many authors from the eighteenth to the early twentieth century and connecting them up with official capital accounts from the late twentieth and early twenty-first century. The other major limitation of official national accounts, apart from their lack of historical perspective, is that they are deliberately concerned only with aggregates and averages and not with distributions and inequalities. We must therefore draw on other sources to measure the distribution of income and wealth and to study inequalities. National accounts thus constitute a crucial element of our analyses, but only when completed with additional historical and distributional data. The Global Distribution of Production I begin by examining the evolution of the global distribution of production, which is relatively well known from the early nineteenth century on. For earlier periods, estimates are more approximate, but we know the broad outlines, thanks most notably to the historical work of Angus Maddison, especially since the overall pattern is relatively simple. From 1900 to 1980, 70–80 percent of the global production of goods and services was concentrated in Europe and America, which incontestably dominated the rest of the world. By 2010, the European–American share had declined to roughly 50 percent, or approximately the same level as in 1860. In all probability, it will continue to fall and may go as low as 20–30 percent at some point in the twenty-first century. This was the level maintained up to the turn of the nineteenth century and would be consistent with the European–American share of the world's population.

From Continental Blocs to Regional Blocs The general pattern just described is well known, but a number of points need to be clarified and refined. First, putting Europe and the Americas together as a single "Western bloc" simplifies the presentation but is largely artificial. Europe attained its maximal economic weight on the eve of World War I, when it accounted for nearly 50 percent of global output, and it has declined steadily since then, whereas America attained its peak in the 1950s, when it accounted for nearly 40 percent of global output. Furthermore, both Europe and the Americas can be broken down into two highly unequal subregions: a hyperdeveloped core and a less developed periphery. Broadly speaking, global inequality is best analyzed in terms of regional blocs rather than continental blocs which shows the distribution of global output in 2012. All these numbers are of no interest in themselves, but it is useful to familiarize oneself with the principal orders of magnitude. The population of the planet is close to 7 billion in 2012, and global output is slightly greater than 70 trillion euros, so that global output per capita is almost exactly 10,000 euros. If we subtract 10 percent for capital depreciation and divide by 12, we find that this yields an average per capita monthly income of 760 euros, which may be a clearer way of making the point. In other words, if global output and the income to which it gives rise were equally divided, each individual in the world would have an income of about 760 euros per month. The population of Europe is about 740 million, about 540 million of whom live in member countries of the European Union, whose per capita output exceeds 27,000 euros per year. The remaining 200 million people live in Russia and Ukraine, where the per capita output is about 15,000 euros per year, barely 50 percent above the global average. The European Union itself is relatively heterogeneous: 410 million of its citizens live in what used to be called Western Europe, threequarters of them in the five most populous countries of the Union, namely Germany, France, Great Britain, Italy, and Spain, with an average per capita GDP of 31,000 euros per year, while the remaining 130 million live in what used to be Eastern Europe, with an average per capita output on the order of 16,000 euros per year, not very different from the Russia-Ukraine bloc. The Americas can also be divided into distinct regions that are even more unequal than the European center and periphery: the US-Canada bloc has 350 million people with a per capita output of 40,000 euros, while Latin America has 600 million people with a per capita output of 10,000 euros, exactly equal to the world average. Sub-Saharan Africa, with a population of 900 million and an annual output of only 1.8 trillion euros (less than the French GDP of 2 trillion), is economically the poorest region of the world, with a per capita output of only 2,000 euros per year. India is slightly higher, while North Africa does markedly better, and China even better than that: with a per capita output of 8,000 euros per year, China in 2012 is not far below the world average. Japan's annual per capita output is equal to that of the wealthiest European countries (approximately 30,000 euros), but its population is such a small minority in the greater Asian population that it has little influence on the continental average, which is close to that of China.

To sum up, global inequality ranges from regions in which the per capita income is on the order of 150–250 euros per month (sub-Saharan Africa, India) to regions where it is as high as 2,500–3,000 euros per month (Western Europe, North America, Japan), that is, ten to twenty times higher. The global average, which is roughly equal to the Chinese average, is around 600–800 euros per month. These orders of magnitude are significant and worth remembering. Bear in mind, however, that the margin of error in these figures is considerable: it is always much more difficult to measure inequalities between countries (or between different periods) than within them. For example, global inequality would be markedly higher if we used current exchange rates rather than purchasing power parities, as I have done thus far. To understand what these terms mean, first consider the euro/dollar exchange rate. In 2012, a euro was worth about $1.30 on the foreign exchange market. A European with an income of 1,000 euros per month could go to his or her bank and exchange that amount for $1,300. If that person then took that money to the United States to spend, his or her purchasing power would be $1,300. But according to the official International Comparison Program (ICP), European prices are about 10 percent higher than American prices, so that if this same European spent the same money in Europe, his or her purchasing power would be closer to an American income of $1,200. Thus we say that $1.20 has "purchasing power parity" with 1 euro. I used this parity rather than the exchange rate to convert American GDP to euros in Table 1.1, and I did the same for the other countries listed. In other words, we compare the GDP of different countries on the basis of the actual purchasing power of their citizens, who generally spend their income at home rather than abroad.

The other advantage of using purchasing power parities is that they are more stable than exchange rates. Indeed, exchange rates reflect not only the supply and demand for the goods and services of different countries but also sudden changes in the investment strategies of international investors and volatile estimates of the political and/or financial stability of this or that country, to say nothing of unpredictable changes in monetary policy. Exchange rates are therefore extremely volatile, as a glance at the large fluctuations of the dollar over the past few decades will show. The dollar/euro rate went from $1.30 per euro in the 1990s to less than $0.90 in 2001 before rising to around $1.50 in 2008 and then falling back to $1.30 in 2012. During that time, the purchasing power parity of the euro rose gently from roughly $1 per euro in the early 1990s to roughly $1.20 in 2010 Despite the best efforts of the international organizations involved in the ICP, there is no escaping the fact that these purchasing power parity estimates are rather uncertain, with margins of error on the order of 10 percent if not higher, even between countries at comparable levels of development. For example, the most recent available survey shows that while some European prices (for energy, housing, hotels, and restaurants) are indeed higher than comparable American prices, others are sharply lower (for health and education, for instance). In theory, the official estimates weight all prices according to the weight of various goods and services in a typical budget for each country, but such calculations clearly leave a good deal of room for error, particularly since it is very hard to 25 26 27 measure qualitative differences for many services. In any case, it is important to emphasize that each of these price indices measures a different aspect of social reality. The price of energy measures purchasing power for energy (which is greater in the United States), while the price of health care measures purchasing power in that area (which is greater in Europe). The reality of inequality between countries is multidimensional, and it is misleading to say that it can all be summed up with a single index leading to an unambiguous classification, especially between countries with fairly similar average incomes. In the poorer countries, the corrections introduced by purchasing power parity are even larger: in Africa and Asia, prices are roughly half what they are in the rich countries, so that GDP roughly doubles when purchasing power parity is used for comparisons rather than the market exchange rate. This is chiefly a result of the fact that the prices of goods and services that cannot be traded internationally are lower, because these are usually relatively labor intensive and involve relatively unskilled labor (a relatively abundant factor of production in less developed countries), as opposed to skilled labor and capital (which are relatively scarce in less developed countries). Broadly speaking, the poorer a country is, the greater the correction: in 2012, the correction coefficient was 1.6 in China and 2.5 in India. At this moment, the euro is worth 8 Chinese yuan on the foreign exchange market but only 5 yuan in purchasing power parity.

Some writers, including Angus Maddison, argue that the gap is not as small as it might appear and that official international statistics underestimate Chinese GDP. Because of the uncertainties surrounding exchange rates and purchasing power parities, the average per capita monthly incomes discussed earlier (150–250 euros for the poorest countries, 600–800 euros for middling countries, and 2,500–3,000 euros for the richest countries) should be treated as approximations rather than mathematical certainties. For example, the share of the rich countries (European Union, United States, Canada, and Japan) in global income was 46 percent in 2012 if we use purchasing power parity but 57 percent if we use current exchange rates. The "truth" probably lies somewhere between these two figures and is probably closer to the first. Still, the orders of magnitude remain the same, as does the fact that the share of income going to the wealthy countries has been declining steadily since the 1970s. Regardless of what measure is used, the world clearly seems to have entered a phase in which rich and poor countries are converging in income.

In fact, it is valid to equate income and output only at the global level and not at the national or continental level. Generally speaking, the global income distribution is more unequal than the output distribution, because the countries with the highest per capita output are also more likely to own part of the capital of other countries and therefore to receive a positive flow of income from capital originating in countries with a lower level of per capita output. In other words, the rich countries are doubly wealthy: they both produce more at home and invest more abroad, so that their national income per head is greater than their output per head. The opposite is true for poor countries. More specifically, all of the major developed countries (the United States, Japan, Germany, France, and Britain) currently enjoy a level of national income that is slightly greater than their domestic product. As noted, however, net income from abroad is just slightly positive and does not radically alter the standard of living in these countries. It amounts to about 1 or 2 percent of GDP in the United States, France, and Britain and 2–3 percent of GDP in Japan and Germany. This is nevertheless a significant boost to national income, especially for Japan and Germany, whose trade surpluses have enabled them to accumulate over the past several decades substantial reserves of foreign capital, the return on which is today considerable. I turn now from the wealthiest countries taken individually to continental blocs taken as a whole. What we find in Europe, America, and Asia is something close to equilibrium: the wealthier countries in each bloc (generally in the north) receive a positive flow of income from capital, which is partly canceled by the flow out of other countries (generally in the south and east), so that at the continental level, total income is almost exactly equal to total output, generally within 0.5 percent. The only continent not in equilibrium is Africa, where a substantial share of capital is owned by foreigners. According to the balance of payments data compiled since 1970 by the United Nations and other international organizations such as the World Bank and International Monetary Fund, the income of Africans is roughly 5 percent less than the continent's output (and as high as 10 percent lower in some individual countries). With capital's share of income at about 30 percent, this means that nearly 20 percent of African capital is owned by foreigners: think of the London stockholders of the Marikana platinum mine discussed at the beginning of this chapter. It is important to realize what such a figure means in practice. Since some kinds of wealth (such as residential real estate and agricultural capital) are rarely owned by foreign investors, it follows that the foreign-owned share of Africa's manufacturing capital may exceed 40–50 percent and may be higher still in other sectors. Despite the fact that there are many imperfections in the balance of payments data, foreign ownership is clearly an important reality in Africa today. 32 33 If we look back farther in time, we find even more marked international imbalances. On the eve of World War I, the national income of Great Britain, the world's leading investor, was roughly 10 percent above its domestic product. The gap was more than 5 percent in France, the number two colonial power and global investor, and Germany was a close third, even though its colonial empire was insignificant, because its highly developed industrial sector accumulated large claims on the rest of the world. British, French, and German investment went partly to other European countries and the United States and partly to Asia and Africa. Overall, the European powers in 1913 owned an estimated one-third to one-half of the domestic capital of Asia and Africa and more than threequarters of their industrial capital. What Forces Favor Convergence? In theory, the fact that the rich countries own part of the capital of poor countries can have virtuous effects by promoting convergence. If the rich countries are so flush with savings and capital that there is little reason to build new housing or add new machinery (in which case economists say that the "marginal productivity of capital," that is, the additional output due to adding one new unit of capital "at the margin," is very low), it can be collectively efficient to invest some part of domestic savings in poorer countries abroad. Thus the wealthy countries—or at any rate the residents of wealthy countries with capital to spare—will obtain a better return on their investment by investing abroad, and the poor countries will increase their productivity and thus close the gap between them and the rich countries. According to classical economic theory, this mechanism, based on the free flow of capital and equalization of the marginal productivity of capital at the global level, should lead to convergence of rich and poor countries and an eventual reduction of inequalities through market forces and competition. This optimistic theory has two major defects, however. First, from a strictly logical point of view, the equalization mechanism does not guarantee global convergence of per capita income. At best it can give rise to convergence of per capita output, provided we assume perfect capital mobility and, even more important, total equality of skill levels and human capital across countries—no small assumption. In any case, the possible convergence of output per head does not imply convergence of income per head. After the wealthy countries have invested in their poorer neighbors, they may continue to own them indefinitely, and indeed their share of ownership may grow to massive proportions, so that the per capita national income of the wealthy countries remains permanently greater than that of the poorer countries, which must continue to pay to foreigners a substantial share of what their citizens produce (as African countries have done for decades). In order to determine how likely such a situation is to arise, we must compare the rate of return on capital that the poor countries must pay to the rich to the growth rates of rich and poor economies. Before proceeding down this road, we must first gain a better understanding of the dynamics of the capital/income ratio within a given country. Furthermore, if we look at the historical record, it does not appear that capital mobility has been the primary factor promoting convergence of rich and poor nations. None of the Asian countries that have moved closer to the developed countries of the West in recent years has benefited from large foreign investments, whether it be Japan, South Korea, or Taiwan and more recently China. In 34 essence, all of these countries themselves financed the necessary investments in physical capital and,even more, in human capital, which the latest research holds to be the key to long-term growth. Conversely, countries owned by other countries, whether in the colonial period or in Africa today,have been less successful, most notably because they have tended to specialize in areas without muchprospect of future development and because they have been subject to chronic political instability. Part of the reason for that instability may be the following. When a country is largely owned byforeigners, there is a recurrent and almost irrepressible social demand for expropriation. Otherpolitical actors respond that investment and development are possible only if existing property rightsare unconditionally protected. The country is thus caught in an endless alternation betweenrevolutionary governments (whose success in improving actual living conditions for their citizens isoften limited) and governments dedicated to the protection of existing property owners, thereby layingthe groundwork for the next revolution or coup. Inequality of capital ownership is already difficult toaccept and peacefully maintain within a single national community. Internationally, it is almostimpossible to sustain without a colonial type of political domination. Make no mistake: participation in the global economy is not negative in itself. Autarky has neverpromoted prosperity. The Asian countries that have lately been catching up with the rest of the worldhave clearly benefited from openness to foreign influences. But they have benefited far more fromopen markets for goods and services and advantageous terms of trade than from free capital flows.China, for example, still imposes controls on capital: foreigners cannot invest in the country freely,but that has not hindered capital accumulation, for which domestic savings largely suffice. Japan,South Korea, and Taiwan all financed investment out of savings. Many studies also show that gainsfrom free trade come mainly from the diffusion of knowledge and from the productivity gains madenecessary by open borders, not from static gains associated with specialization, which appear to befairly modest. To sum up, historical experience suggests that the principal mechanism for convergence at theinternational as well as the domestic level is the diffusion of knowledge. In other words, the poorcatch up with the rich to the extent that they achieve the same level of technological know-how, skill,and education, not by becoming the property of the wealthy. The diffusion of knowledge is not likemanna from heaven: it is often hastened by international openness and trade (autarky does notencourage technological transfer). Above all, knowledge diffusion depends on a country's ability tomobilize financing as well as institutions that encourage large-scale investment in education andtraining of the population while guaranteeing a stable legal framework that various economic actorscan reliably count on. It is therefore closely associated with the achievement of legitimate andefficient government. Concisely stated, these are the main lessons that history has to teach aboutglobal growth and international inequalities.

CHAPTER TWO

Growth: Illusions and Realities

A global convergence process in which emerging countries are catching up with developed countries seems well under way today, even though substantial inequalities between rich and poor countries remain. There is, moreover, no evidence that this catch-up process is primarily a result of investment by the rich countries in the poor. Indeed, the contrary is true: past experience shows that the promise of a good outcome is greater when poor countries are able to invest in themselves. Beyond the central issue of convergence, however, the point I now want to stress is that the twenty-first century may see a return to a low-growth regime. More precisely, what we will find is that growth has in fact always been relatively slow except in exceptional periods or when catch-up is occurring. Furthermore, all signs are that growth—or at any rate its demographic component—will be even slower in the future. To understand what is at issue here and its relation to the convergence process and the dynamics of inequality, it is important to decompose the growth of output into two terms: population growth and per capita output growth. In other words, growth always includes a purely demographic component and a purely economic component, and only the latter allows for an improvement in the standard of living. In public debate this decomposition is too often forgotten, as many people seem to assume that population growth has ceased entirely, which is not yet the case—far from it, actually, although all signs indicate that we are headed slowly in that direction. In 2013–2014, for example, global economic growth will probably exceed 3 percent, thanks to very rapid progress in the emerging countries. But global population is still growing at an annual rate close to 1 percent, so that global output per capita is actually growing at a rate barely above 2 percent (as is global income per capita). Growth over the Very Long Run Before turning to present trends, I will go back in time and present the stages and orders of magnitude of global growth since the Industrial

Revolution.

Several important facts stand out. First, the takeoff in growth that began in the eighteenth century involved relatively modest annual growth rates. Second, the demographic and economic components of growth were roughly similar in magnitude. According to the best available estimates, global output grew at an average annual rate of 1.6 percent between 1700 and 2012, 0.8 percent of which reflects population growth, while another 0.8 percent came fromgrowth in output per head. Such growth rates may seem low compared to what one often hears in current debates, where annual growth rates below 1 percent are frequently dismissed as insignificant and it is commonly assumed that real growth doesn't begin until one has achieved 3–4 percent a year or even more, as Europe did in the thirty years after World War II and as China is doing today. In fact, however, growth on the order of 1 percent a year in both population and per capita output, if continued over a very long period of time, as was the case after 1700, is extremely rapid, especially when compared with the virtually zero growth rate that we observe in the centuries prior to the Industrial Revolution.

We see clearly how different choices of time frame lead to contradictory perceptions of the growth process. Over a period of one year, 1 percent growth seems very low, almost imperceptible. People living at the time might not notice any change at all. To them, such growth might seem like complete stagnation, in which each year is virtually identical to the previous one. Growth might therefore seemlike a fairly abstract notion, a purely mathematical and statistical construct. But if we expand the time frame to that of a generation, that is, about thirty years, which is the most relevant time scale for evaluating change in the society we live in, the same growth rate results in an increase of about a third, which represents a transformation of quite substantial magnitude. Although this is less impressive than growth of 2–2.5 percent per year, which leads to a doubling in every generation, it is still enough to alter society regularly and profoundly and in the very long run to transform it radically. The law of cumulative growth is essentially identical to the law of cumulative returns, which says that an annual rate of return of a few percent, compounded over several decades, automatically results in a very large increase of the initial capital, provided that the return is constantly reinvested, or at a minimum that only a small portion of it is consumed by the owner of the capital (small in comparison with the growth rate of the society in question).

Negative Demographic Growth?

These forecasts are obviously rather uncertain. They depend first on the evolution of life expectancy (and thus in part on advances in medical science) and second on the decisions that future generations will make in regard to childbearing. If life expectancy is taken as given, the fertility rate determines the demographic growth rate. The important point to bear in mind is that small variations in the number of children couples decide to have can have significant consequences for society writ large. What demographic history teaches us is that these childbearing decisions are largely unpredictable. They are influenced by cultural, economic, psychological, and personal factors related to the life goals that individuals choose for themselves. These decisions may also depend on the material conditions that different countries decide to provide, or not provide, for the purpose of making family life compatible with professional life: schools, day care, gender equality, and so on. These issues will undoubtedly play a growing part in twenty-first-century political debate and public policy. Looking beyond the general schema just outlined, we find numerous regional differences and stunning changes in demographic patterns, many of them linked to specific features of each country's history. The most spectacular reversal no doubt involves Europe and America. In 1780, when the population of Western Europe was already greater than 100 million and that of North America barely 3 million, no one could have guessed the magnitude of the change that lay ahead. By 2010, the population of Western Europe was just above 410 million, while the North American population had increased to 350 million. According to UN projections, the catch-up process will be complete by 2050, at which time the Western European population will have grown to around 430 million, compared with 450 million for North America. What explains this reversal? Not just the flow of immigrants to the New World but also the markedly higher fertility rate there compared with old Europe. The gap persists to this day, even among groups that came originally from Europe, and the reasons for it remain largely a mystery to demographers. One thing is sure: the higher fertility rate in North America is not due to more generous family policies, since such policies are virtually nonexistent there. Should the difference be interpreted as reflecting a greater North American faith in the future, a New World optimism, and a greater propensity to think of one's own and one's children's futures in terms of a perpetually growing economy? When it comes to decisions as complex as those related to fertility, no psychological or cultural explanation can be ruled out in advance, and anything is possible. Indeed, US demographic growth has been declining steadily, and current trends could be reversed if immigration into the European Union continues to increase, or fertility increases, or the European life expectancy widens the gap with the United States. United Nations forecasts are not certainties. We also find spectacular demographic turnarounds within each continent. France was the most populous country in Europe in the eighteenth century (and, as noted, both Young and Malthus saw this as the reason for French rural poverty and even as the cause of the French Revolution). But the 4 5 demographic transition occurred unusually early in France: a fall in the birth rate led to a virtually stagnant population as early as the nineteenth century. This is generally attributed to deChristianization, which also came early. Yet an equally unusual leap in the birth rate took place in the twentieth century—a leap often attributed to pronatal policies adopted after the two world wars and to the trauma of defeat in 1940. France's wager may well pay off, since UN forecasts predict that the population of France will exceed that of Germany by 2050 or so. It is difficult, however, to distinguish the various causes of this reversal: economic, political, cultural, and psychological factors all play a part. On a grander scale, everyone knows the consequences of the Chinese policy to allow only one child per family (a decision made in the 1970s, when China feared being condemned to remain an underdeveloped country, and now in the process of being relaxed). The Chinese population, which was roughly 50 percent greater than India's when this radical policy was adopted, is now close to being surpassed by that of its neighbor. According to the United Nations, India will be the most populous country in the world by 2020. Yet here, too, nothing is set in stone: population history invariably combines individual choices, developmental strategies, and national psychologies—private motives and power motives. No one at this point can seriously claim to know what demographic turnarounds may occur in the twenty-first century. It would therefore be presumptuous to regard the official UN predictions as anything other than a "central scenario." In any case, the United Nations has also published two other sets of predictions, and the gaps between these various scenarios at the 2100 horizon are, unsurprisingly, quite large. The central scenario is nevertheless the most plausible we have, given the present state of our knowledge. Between 1990 and 2012, the population of Europe was virtually stagnant, and the population of several countries actually decreased. Fertility rates in Germany, Italy, Spain, and Poland fell below 1.5 children per woman in the 2000s, and only an increase in life expectancy coupled with a high level of immigration prevented a rapid decrease of population. In view of these facts, the UN prediction of zero demographic growth in Europe until 2030 and slightly negative rates after that is by no means extravagant. Indeed, it seems to be the most reasonable forecast. The same is true for UN predictions for Asia and other regions: the generations being born now in Japan and China are roughly one-third smaller than the generations born in the 1990s. The demographic transition is largely complete. Changes in individual decisions and government policies may slightly alter these trends: for example, slightly negative rates (such as we see in Japan and Germany) may become slightly positive (as in France and Scandinavia), which would be a significant change, but we are unlikely to see anything more than that, at least for the next several decades. Of course the very long-run forecasts are much more uncertain. Note, however, that if the rate of population growth observed from 1700 to 2012—0.8 percent per year—were to continue for the next three centuries, the world's population would be on the order of 70 billion in 2300. To be sure, this cannot be ruled out: childbearing behavior could change, or technological advances might allow growth with much less pollution than is possible to imagine now, with output consisting of new, almost entirely nonmaterial goods and services produced with renewable energy sources exhibiting a negligible carbon footprint. At this point, however, it is hardly an exaggeration to say that a world population of 70 billion seems neither especially plausible nor particularly desirable. The most likely 6 7 hypothesis is that the global population growth rate over the next several centuries will be significantly less than 0.8 percent. The official prediction of 0.1–0.2 percent per year over the very long run seems rather plausible a priori. Growth as a Factor for Equalization In any case, it is not the purpose of this book to make demographic predictions but rather to acknowledge these various possibilities and analyze their implications for the evolution of the wealth distribution. Beyond the consequences for the development and relative power of nations, demographic growth also has important implications for the structure of inequality. Other things being equal, strong demographic growth tends to play an equalizing role because it decreases the importance of inherited wealth: every generation must in some sense construct itself.

To take an extreme example, in a world in which each couple has ten children, it is clearly better as a general rule not to count too much on inherited wealth, because the family wealth will be divided by ten with each new generation. In such a society, the overall influence of inherited wealth would be strongly diminished, and most people would be more realistic to rely on their own labor and savings. The same would be true in a society where the population is constantly replenished by immigration from other countries, as was the case in America. Assuming that most immigrants arrive without much wealth, the amount of wealth passed down from previous generations is inherently fairly limited in comparison with new wealth accumulated through savings. Demographic growth via immigration has other consequences, however, especially in regard to inequality between immigrants and natives as well as within each group. Such a society is thus not globally comparable to a society in which the primary source of population growth is natural increase (that is, from new births). I will show that the intuition concerning the effects of strong demographic growth can to a certain extent be generalized to societies with very rapid economic (and not just demographic) growth. For example, in a society where output per capita grows tenfold every generation, it is better to count on what one can earn and save from one's own labor: the income of previous generations is so small compared with current income that the wealth accumulated by one's parents and grandparents doesn't amount to much. Conversely, a stagnant or, worse, decreasing population increases the influence of capital accumulated in previous generations. The same is true of economic stagnation. With low growth, moreover, it is fairly plausible that the rate of return on capital will be substantially higher than the growth rate, a situation that, as I noted in the introduction, is the main factor leading toward very substantial inequality in the distribution of wealth over the long run. Capital-dominated societies in the past, with hierarchies largely determined by inherited wealth (a category that includes both traditional rural societies and the countries of nineteenth-century Europe) can arise and subsist only in low-growth regimes. I will consider the extent to which the probable return to a low-growth regime, if it occurs, will affect the dynamics of capital accumulation and the structure of inequality. In particular, inherited wealth will make a comeback—a long-term phenomenon whose effects are already being felt in Europe and that could extend to other parts of the world as well. That is why it is important for present purposes to become familiar with the history of demographic and economic growth. There is another mechanism whereby growth can contribute to the reduction of inequality, or at least to a more rapid circulation of elites, which must also be discussed. This mechanism is potentially complementary to the first, although it is less important and more ambiguous. When growth is zero or very low, the various economic and social functions as well as types of professional activity, are reproduced virtually without change from generation to generation. By contrast, constant growth, even if it is only 0.5 or 1 or 1.5 percent per year, means that new functions are constantly being created and new skills are needed in every generation. Insofar as tastes and capabilities are only partially transmitted from generation to generation (or are transmitted much less automatically and mechanically than capital in land, real estate, or financial assets are transmitted by inheritance), growth can thus increase social mobility for individuals whose parents did not belong to the elite of the previous generation. This increased social mobility need not imply decreased income inequality, but in theory it does limit the reproduction and amplification of inequalities of wealth and therefore over the long run also limits income inequality to a certain extent. One should be wary, however, of the conventional wisdom that modern economic growth is a marvelous instrument for revealing individual talents and aptitudes. There is some truth in this view, but since the early nineteenth century it has all too often been used to justify inequalities of all sorts, no matter how great their magnitude and no matter what their real causes may be, while at the same time gracing the winners in the new industrial economy with every imaginable virtue. For instance, the liberal economist Charles Dunoyer, who served as a prefect under the July Monarchy, had this to say in his 1845 book De la liberté du travail (in which he of course expressed his opposition to any form of labor law or social legislation): "one consequence of the industrial regime is to destroy artificial inequalities, but this only highlights natural inequalities all the more clearly." For Dunoyer, natural inequalities included differences in physical, intellectual, and moral capabilities, differences that were crucial to the new economy of growth and innovation that he saw wherever he looked. This was his reason for rejecting state intervention of any kind: "superior abilities ... are the source of everything that is great and useful.... Reduce everything to equality and you will bring everything to a standstill." One sometimes hears the same thought expressed today in the idea that the new information economy will allow the most talented individuals to increase their productivity many times over. The plain fact is that this argument is often used to justify extreme inequalities and to defend the privileges of the winners without much consideration for the losers, much less for the facts, and without any real effort to verify whether this very convenient principle can actually explain the changes we observe. I will come back to this point. The Stages of Economic Growth I turn now to the growth of per capita output. As noted, this was of the same order as population growth over the period 1700–2012: 0.8 percent per year on average, which equates to a multiplication of output by a factor of roughly ten over three centuries. Average global per capita income is currently around 760 euros per month; in 1700, it was less than 70 euros per month, roughly equal to income in the poorest countries of Sub-Saharan Africa in 2012. This comparison is suggestive, but its significance should not be exaggerated. When comparing very different societies and periods, we must avoid trying to sum everything up with a single figure, 8 9 for example "the standard of living in society A is ten times higher than in society B." When growth attains levels such as these, the notion of per capita output is far more abstract than that of population, which at least corresponds to a tangible reality (it is much easier to count people than to count goods and services). Economic development begins with the diversification of ways of life and types of goods and services produced and consumed. It is thus a multidimensional process whose very nature makes it impossible to sum up properly with a single monetary index. Take the wealthy countries as an example. In Western Europe, North America, and Japan, average per capita income increased from barely 100 euros per month in 1700 to more than 2,500 euros per month in 2012, a more than twentyfold increase. The increase in productivity, or output per hour worked, was even greater, because each person's average working time decreased dramatically: as the developed countries grew wealthier, they decided to work less in order to allow for more free time (the work day grew shorter, vacations grew longer, and so on). Much of this spectacular growth occurred in the twentieth century. Globally, the average growth of per capita output of 0.8 percent over the period 1700–2012 breaks down as follows: growth of barely 0.1 percent in the eighteenth century, 0.9 percent in the nineteenth century, and 1.6 percent in the twentieth century (see Table 2.1). In Western Europe, average growth of 1.0 percent in the same period breaks down as 0.2 percent in the eighteenth century, 1.1 percent in the nineteenth century, and 1.9 percent in the twentieth century. Average purchasing power in Europe barely increased at all from 1700 to 1820, then more than doubled between 1820 and 1913, and increased more than sixfold between 1913 and 2012. Basically, the eighteenth century suffered from the same economic stagnation as previous centuries. The nineteenth century witnessed the first sustained growth in per capita output, although large segments of the population derived little benefit from this, at least until the last three decades of the century. It was not until the twentieth century that economic growth became a tangible, unmistakable reality for everyone. Around the turn of the twentieth century, average per capita income in Europe stood at just under 400 euros per month, compared with 2,500 euros in 2010. But what does it mean for purchasing power to be multiplied by a factor of twenty, ten, or even six? It clearly does not mean that Europeans in 2012 produced and consumed six times more goods and services than they produced and consumed in 1913. For example, average food consumption obviously did not increase sixfold. Basic dietary needs would long since have been satisfied if consumption had increased that much. Not only in Europe but everywhere, improvements in purchasing power and standard of living over the long run depend primarily on a transformation of the structure of consumption: a consumer basket initially filled mainly with foodstuffs gradually gave way to a much more diversified basket of goods, rich in manufactured products and services. Furthermore, even if Europeans in 2012 wished to consume six times the amount of goods and services they consumed in 1913, they could not: some prices have risen more rapidly than the "average" price, while others have risen more slowly, so that purchasing power has not increased sixfold for all types of goods and services. In the short run, the problem of "relative prices" can be neglected, and it is reasonable to assume that the indices of "average" prices published by government agencies allow us to correctly gauge changes in purchasing power. In the long run, however, relative prices shift dramatically, as does the composition of the typical consumer's basket of goods, owing largely to the advent of new goods and services, so that average price indices fail to 10 11 12 give an accurate picture of the changes that have taken place, no matter how sophisticated the techniques used by the statisticians to process the many thousands of prices they monitor and to correct for improvements in product quality. What Does a Tenfold Increase in Purchasing Power Mean? In fact, the only way to accurately gauge the spectacular increase in standards of living since the Industrial Revolution is to look at income levels in today's currency and compare these to price levels for the various goods and services available in different periods. For now, I will simply summarize the main lessons derived from such an exercise. It is standard to distinguish the following three types of goods and services. For industrial goods, productivity growth has been more rapid than for the economy as a whole, so that prices in this sector have fallen relative to the average of all prices. Foodstuffs is a sector in which productivity has increased continuously and crucially over the very long run (thereby allowing a greatly increased population to be fed by ever fewer hands, liberating a growing portion of the workforce for other tasks), even though the increase in productivity has been less rapid in the agricultural sector than in the industrial sector, so that food prices have evolved at roughly the same rate as the average of all prices. Finally, productivity growth in the service sector has generally been low (or even zero in some cases, which explains why this sector has tended to employ a steadily increasing share of the workforce), so that the price of services has increased more rapidly than the average of all prices. This general pattern is well known. Although it is broadly speaking correct, it needs to be refined and made more precise. In fact, there is a great deal of diversity within each of these three sectors. The prices of many food items did in fact evolve at the same rate as the average of all prices. For example, in France, the price of a kilogram of carrots evolved at the same rate as the overall price index in the period 1900–2010, so that purchasing power expressed in terms of carrots evolved in the same way as average purchasing power (which increased approximately sixfold). An average worker could afford slightly less than ten kilos of carrots per day at the turn of the twentieth century, while he could afford nearly sixty kilos per day at the turn of the twenty-first century. For other foodstuffs, however, such as milk, butter, eggs, and dairy products in general, major technological advances in processing, manufacturing, conservation, and so on led to relative price decreases and thus to increases in purchasing power greater than sixfold. The same is true for products that benefited fromthe significant reduction in transport costs over the course of the twentieth century: for example, French purchasing power expressed in terms of oranges increased tenfold, and expressed in terms of bananas, twentyfold. Conversely, purchasing power measured in kilos of bread or meat rose less than fourfold, although there was a sharp increase in the quality and variety of products on offer. Manufactured goods present an even more mixed picture, primarily because of the introduction of radically new goods and spectacular improvements in performance. The example often cited in recent years is that of electronics and computer technology. Advances in computers and cell phones in the 1990s and of tablets and smartphones in the 2000s and beyond have led to tenfold increases in purchasing power in a very short period of time: prices have fallen by half, while performance has increased by a factor of 5. It is important to note that equally impressive examples can be found throughout the long history of 13 14 industrial development. Take the bicycle. In France in the 1880s, the cheapest model listed in catalogs and sales brochures cost the equivalent of six months of the average worker's wage. And this was a relatively rudimentary bicycle, "which had wheels covered with just a strip of solid rubber and only one brake that pressed directly against the front rim." Technological progress made it possible to reduce the price to one month's wages by 1910. Progress continued, and by the 1960s one could buy a quality bicycle (with "detachable wheel, two brakes, chain and mud guards, saddle bags, lights, and reflector") for less than a week's average wage. All in all, and leaving aside the prodigious improvement in the quality and safety of the product, purchasing power in terms of bicycles rose by a factor of 40 between 1890 and 1970. One could easily multiply examples by comparing the price history of electric light bulbs, household appliances, table settings, clothing, and automobiles to prevailing wages in both developed and emerging economies. All of these examples show how futile and reductive it is to try to sum up all these change with a single index, as in "the standard of living increased tenfold between date A and date B." When family budgets and lifestyles change so radically and purchasing power varies so much from one good to another, it makes little sense to take averages, because the result depends heavily on the weights and measures of quality one chooses, and these are fairly uncertain, especially when one is attempting comparisons across several centuries. None of this in any way challenges the reality of growth. Quite the contrary: the material conditions of life have clearly improved dramatically since the Industrial Revolution, allowing people around the world to eat better, dress better, travel, learn, obtain medical care, and so on. It remains interesting to measure growth rates over shorter periods such as a generation or two. Over a period of thirty to sixty years, there are significant differences between a growth rate of 0.1 percent per year (3 percent per generation), 1 percent per year (35 percent per generation), or 3 percent per year (143 percent per generation). It is only when growth statistics are compiled over very long periods leading to multiplications by huge factors that the numbers lose a part of their significance and become relatively abstract and arbitrary quantities. Growth: A Diversification of Lifestyles To conclude this discussion, consider the case of services, where diversity is probably the most extreme. In theory, things are fairly clear: productivity growth in the service sector has been less rapid, so that purchasing power expressed in terms of services has increased much less. As a typical case—a "pure" service benefiting from no major technological innovation over the centuries—one often takes the example of barbers: a haircut takes just as long now as it did a century ago, so that the price of a haircut has increased by the same factor as the barber's pay, which has itself progressed at the same rate as the average wage and average income (to a first approximation). In other words, an hour's work of the typical wage-earner in the twenty-first century can buy just as many haircuts as an hour's work a hundred years ago, so that purchasing power expressed in terms of haircuts has not increased (and may in fact have decreased slightly). In fact, the diversity of services is so extreme that the very notion of a service sector makes little sense. The decomposition of the economy into three sectors—primary, secondary, and tertiary—was 15 16 an idea of the mid-twentieth century in societies where each sector included similar, or at any rate comparable, fractions of economic activity and the workforce . But once 70–80 percent of the workforce in the developed countries found itself working in the service sector, the category ceased to have the same meaning: it provided little information about the nature of the trades and services produced in a given society. In order to find our way through this vast aggregate of activities, whose growth accounts for much of the improvement in living conditions since the nineteenth century, it will be useful to distinguish several subsectors. Consider first services in health and education, which by themselves account for more than 20 percent of total employment in the most advanced countries (or as much as all industrial sectors combined). There is every reason to think that this fraction will continue to increase, given the pace of medical progress and the steady growth of higher education. The number of jobs in retail; hotels, cafés, and restaurants; and culture and leisure activities also increased rapidly, typically accounting for 20 percent of total employment. Services to firms (consulting, accounting, design, data processing, etc.) combined with real estate and financial services (real estate agencies, banks, insurance, etc.) and transportation add another 20 percent of the job total. If you then add government and security services (general administration, courts, police, armed forces, etc.), which account for nearly 10 percent of total employment in most countries, you reach the 70–80 percent figure given in official statistics.

Note that an important part of these services, especially in health and education, is generally financed by taxes and provided free of charge. The details of financing vary from country to country, as does the exact share financed by taxes, which is higher in Europe, for example, than in the United States or Japan. Still, it is quite high in all developed countries: broadly speaking, at least half of the total cost of health and education services is paid for by taxes, and in a number of European countries it is more than three-quarters. This raises potential new difficulties and uncertainties when it comes to measuring and comparing increases in the standard of living in different countries over the long run. This is not a minor point: not only do these two sectors account for more than 20 percent of GDP and employment in the most advanced countries—a percentage that will no doubt increase in the future—but health and education probably account for the most tangible and impressive improvement in standards of living over the past two centuries. Instead of living in societies where the life expectancy 17 was barely forty years and nearly everyone was illiterate, we now live in societies where it is common to reach the age of eighty and everyone has at least minimal access to culture. In national accounts, the value of public services available to the public for free is always estimated on the basis of the production costs assumed by the government, that is, ultimately, by taxpayers. These costs include the wages paid to health workers and teachers employed by hospitals, schools, and public universities. This method of valuing services has its flaws, but it is logically consistent and clearly more satisfactory than simply excluding free public services from GDP calculations and concentrating solely on commodity production. It would be economically absurd to leave public services out entirely, because doing so would lead in a totally artificial way to an underestimate of the GDP and national income of a country that chose a public system of health and education rather than a private system, even if the available services were strictly identical. The method used to compute national accounts has the virtue of correcting this bias. Still, it is not perfect. In particular, there is no objective measure of the quality of services rendered (although various correctives for this are under consideration). For example, if a private health insurance system costs more than a public system but does not yield truly superior quality (as a comparison of the United States with Europe suggests), then

GDP will be artificially overvalued in countries that rely mainly on private insurance. Note, too, that the convention in national accounting is not to count any remuneration for public capital such as hospital buildings and equipment or schools and universities. The consequence of this is that a country that privatized its health and education services would see its GDP rise artificially, even if the services produced and the wages paid to employees remained exactly the same. It may be that this method of accounting by costs underestimates the fundamental "value" of education and health and therefore the growth achieved during periods of rapid expansion of services in these areas. Hence there is no doubt that economic growth led to a significant improvement in standard of living over the long run. The best available estimates suggest that global per capita income increased by a factor of more than 10 between 1700 and 2012 (from 70 euros to 760 euros per month) and by a factor of more than 20 in the wealthiest countries (from 100 to 2,500 euros per month). Given the difficulties of measuring such radical transformations, especially if we try to sum them up with a single index, we must be careful not to make a fetish of the numbers, which should rather be taken as indications of orders of magnitude and nothing more.

CHAPTER THREE

The Metamorphoses of Capital

the basic concepts of income and capital and reviewed the main stages of income and output growth since the Industrial Revolution. In this part, I am going to concentrate on the evolution of the capital stock, looking at both its overall size, as measured by the capital/income ratio, and its breakdown into different types of assets, whose nature has changed radically since the eighteenth century. I will consider various forms of wealth (land, buildings, machinery, firms, stocks, bonds, patents, livestock, gold, natural resources, etc.) and examine their development over time, starting with Great Britain and France, the countries about which we possess the most information over the long run. But first I want to take a brief detour through literature, which in the cases of Britain and France offers a very good introduction to the subject of wealth. The Nature of Wealth: From Literature to Reality When Honoré de Balzac and Jane Austen wrote their novels at the beginning of the nineteenth century, the nature of wealth was relatively clear to all readers. Wealth seemed to exist in order to produce rents, that is, dependable, regular payments to the owners of certain assets, which usually took the form of land or government bonds. Père Goriot owned the latter, while the small estate of the Rastignacs consisted of the former. The vast Norland estate that John Dashwood inherits in Sense and Sensibility is also agricultural land, from which he is quick to expel his half-sisters Elinor and Marianne, who must make do with the interest on the small capital in government bonds left to themby their father. In the classic novels of the nineteenth century, wealth is everywhere, and no matter how large or small the capital, or who owns it, it generally takes one of two forms: land or government bonds. From the perspective of the twenty-first century, these types of assets may seem old-fashioned, and it is tempting to consign them to the remote and supposedly vanished past, unconnected with the economic and social realities of the modern era, in which capital is supposedly more "dynamic." Indeed, the characters in nineteenth-century novels often seem like archetypes of the rentier, a suspect figure in the modern era of democracy and meritocracy. Yet what could be more natural to ask of a capital asset than that it produce a reliable and steady income: that is in fact the goal of a "perfect" capital market as economists define it. It would be quite wrong, in fact, to assume that the study of nineteenth-century capital has nothing to teach us today. When we take a closer look, the differences between the nineteenth and twenty-first centuries are less apparent than they might seem at first glance. In the first place, the two types of capital asset—land and government bonds—raise very different issues and probably should not be added together as cavalierly as nineteenth-century novelists did for narrative convenience. Ultimately, a government bond is nothing more than a claim of one portion of the population (those who receive interest) on another (those who pay taxes): it should therefore be excluded from national wealth and included solely in private wealth. The complex question of government debt and the nature of the wealth associated with it is no less important today than it was in 1800, and by studying the past we can learn a lot about an issue of great contemporary concern. Although today's public debt is nowhere near the astronomical levels attained at the beginning of the nineteenth century, at least in Britain, it is at or near a historical record in France and many other countries and is probably the source of as much confusion today as in the Napoleonic era. The process of financial intermediation (whereby individuals deposit money in a bank, which then invests it elsewhere) has become so complex that people are often unaware of who owns what. To be sure, we are in debt. How can we possibly forget it, when the media remind us every day? But to whom exactly do we owe money? In the nineteenth century, the rentiers who lived off the public debt were clearly identified. Is that still the case today? This mystery needs to be dispelled, and studying the past can help us do so. There is also another, even more important complication: many other forms of capital, some of them quite "dynamic," played an essential role not only in classic novels but in the society of the time. After starting out as a noodle maker, Père Goriot made his fortune as a pasta manufacturer and grain merchant. During the wars of the revolutionary and Napoleonic eras, he had an unrivaled eye for the best flour and a knack for perfecting pasta production technologies and setting up distribution networks and warehouses so that he could deliver the right product to the right place at the right time. Only after making a fortune as an entrepreneur did he sell his share of the business, much in the manner of a twenty-first-century startup founder exercising his stock options and pocketing his capital gains. Goriot then invested the proceeds in safer assets: perpetual government bonds that paid interest indefinitely. With this capital he was able to arrange good marriages for his daughters and secure an eminent place for them in Parisian high society. On his deathbed in 1821, abandoned by his daughters Delphine and Anastasie, old Goriot still dreamt of juicy investments in the pasta business in Odessa. César Birotteau, another Balzac character, made his money in perfumes. He was the ingenious inventor of any number of beauty products—Sultan's Cream, Carminative Water, and so on—that Balzac tells us were all the rage in late imperial and Restoration France. But this was not enough for him: when the time came to retire, he sought to triple his capital by speculating boldly on real estate in the neighborhood of La Madeleine, which was developing rapidly in the 1820s. After rejecting the sage advice of his wife, who urged him to invest in good farmland near Chinon and government bonds, he ended in ruin. Jane Austen's heroes were more rural than Balzac's. Prosperous landowners all, they were nevertheless wiser than Balzac's characters in appearance only. In Mansfield Park, Fanny's uncle, Sir Thomas, has to travel out to the West Indies for a year with his eldest son for the purpose of managing his affairs and investments. After returning to Mansfield, he is obliged to set out once again for the islands for a period of many months. In the early 1800s it was by no means simple to manage plantations several thousand miles away. Tending to one's wealth was not a tranquil matter of collecting rent on land or interest on government debt. So which was it: quiet capital or risky investments? Is it safe to conclude that nothing has really changed since 1800? What actual changes have occurred in the structure of capital since the eighteenth century? Père Goriot's pasta may have become Steve Jobs's tablet, and investments in the West Indies in 1800 may have become investments in China or South Africa in 2010, but has the deep structure of capital really changed? Capital is never quiet: it is always risk-oriented and entrepreneurial, at least at its inception, yet it always tends to transform itself into rents as it accumulates in large enough amounts—that is its vocation, its logical destination. What, then, gives us the vague sense that social inequality today is very different from social inequality in the age of Balzac and Austen? Is this just empty talk with no purchase on reality, or can we identify objective factors to explain why some people think that modern capital has become more "dynamic" and less "rent-seeking?"

We find, to begin with, that the capital/income ratio followed quite similar trajectories in both countries, remaining relatively stable in the eighteenth and nineteenth centuries, followed by an enormous shock in the twentieth century, before returning to levels similar to those observed on the eve of World War I. In both Britain and France, the total value of national capital fluctuated between six and seven years of national income throughout the eighteenth and nineteenth centuries, up to 1914. Then, after World War I, the capital/income ratio suddenly plummeted, and it continued to fall during the Depression and World War II, to the point where national capital amounted to only two or three years of national income in the 1950s. The capital/income ratio then began to climb and has continued to do so ever since. In both countries, the total value of national capital in 2010 is roughly five to six years' worth of national income, indeed a bit more than six in France, compared with less than four in the 1980s and barely more than two in the 1950s. The measurements are of course not perfectly precise, but the general shape of the curve is clear. In short, what we see over the course of the century just past is an impressive "U-shaped curve." The capital/income ratio fell by nearly two-thirds between 1914 and 1945 and then more than doubled in the period 1945–2012. These are very large swings, commensurate with the violent military, political, and economic conflicts that marked the twentieth century. Capital, private property, and the global distribution of wealth were key issues in these conflicts. The eighteenth and nineteenth centuries look tranquil by comparison. In the end, by 2010, the capital/income ratio had returned to its pre–World War I level—or even surpassed it if we divide the capital stock by disposable household income rather than national income (a dubious methodological choice, as will be shown later). In any case, regardless of the imperfections and uncertainties of the available measures, there can be no doubt that Britain and France in the 1990s and 2000s regained a level of wealth not seen since the early twentieth century, at the conclusion of a process that originated in the 1950s. By the middle of the twentieth century, capital had largely disappeared. A little more than half a century later, it seems about to return to levels equal to those observed in the eighteenth and nineteenth centuries. Wealth is once again flourishing. Broadly speaking, it was the wars of the twentieth century that wiped away the past to create the illusion that capitalism had been structurally transformed.

National capital = farmland + housing + other domestic capital + net foreign capital A glance at these graphs shows that at the beginning of the eighteenth century, the total value of farmland represented four to five years of national income, or nearly two-thirds of total national capital. Three centuries later, farmland was worth less than 10 percent of national income in both France and Britain and accounted for less than 2 percent of total wealth. This impressive change is hardly surprising: agriculture in the eighteenth century accounted for nearly three-quarters of all economic activity and employment, compared with just a few percent today. It is therefore natural that the share of capital involved in agriculture has evolved in a similar direction. This collapse in the value of farmland (proportionate to national income and national capital) was counterbalanced on the one hand by a rise in the value of housing, which rose from barely one year of national income in the eighteenth century to more than three years today, and on the other hand by an increase in the value of other domestic capital, which rose by roughly the same amount (actually slightly less, from 1.5 years of national income in the eighteenth century to a little less than 3 years today). This very long-term structural transformation reflects on the one hand the growing importance of housing, not only in size but also in quality and value, in the process of economic and industrial development; and on the other the very substantial accumulation since the Industrial Revolution of buildings used for business purposes, infrastructure, machinery, warehouses, offices, tools, and other material and immaterial capital, all of which is used by firms and government organizations to produce all sorts of nonagricultural goods and services. The nature of capital has changed: it once was mainly land but has become primarily housing plus industrial and financial assets. Yet it has lost none of its importance. The Rise and Fall of Foreign Capital What about foreign capital? In Britain and France, it evolved in a very distinctive way, shaped by the turbulent history of these two leading colonial powers over the past three centuries. The net assets these two countries owned in the rest of the world increased steadily during the eighteenth and nineteenth centuries and attained an extremely high level on the eve of World War I, before literally collapsing in the period 1914–1945 and stabilizing at a relatively low level since then, as Figures 3.1 and 3.2 show. Foreign possessions first became important in the period 1750–1800, as we know, for instance, from

Sir Thomas's investments in the West Indies in Jane Austen's Mansfield Park. But the share of foreign assets remained modest: when Austen wrote her novel in 1812, they represented, as far as we can tell from the available sources, barely 10 percent of Britain's national income, or one-thirtieth of the value of agricultural land (which amounted to more than three years of national income). Hence it comes as no surprise to discover that most of Austen's characters lived on the rents from their rural properties. It was during the nineteenth century that British subjects began to accumulate considerable assets in the rest of the world, in amounts previously unknown and never surpassed to this day. By the eve of World War I, Britain had assembled the world's preeminent colonial empire and owned foreign assets equivalent to nearly two years of national income, or 6 times the total value of British farmland (which at that point was worth only 30 percent of national income). Clearly, the structure of wealth had been utterly transformed since the time of Mansfield Park, and one has to hope that Austen's heroes and their descendants were able to adjust in time and follow Sir Thomas's lead by investing a portion of their land rents abroad. By the turn of the twentieth century, capital invested abroad was yielding around 5 percent a year in dividends, interest, and rent, so that British national income was about 10 percent higher than its domestic product. A fairly significant social group were able to live off this boon. France, which commanded the second most important colonial empire, was in a scarcely less enviable situation: it had accumulated foreign assets worth more than a year's national income, so that in the first decade of the twentieth century its national income was 5–6 percent higher than its domestic product. This was equal to the total industrial output of the northern and eastern départements, and it came to France in the form of dividends, interest, royalties, rents, and other revenue on assets that French citizens owned in the country's foreign possessions. 1 2 3 4 5 It is important to understand that these very large net positions in foreign assets allowed Britain and France to run structural trade deficits in the late nineteenth and early twentieth century. Between 1880 and 1914, both countries received significantly more in goods and services from the rest of the world than they exported themselves (their trade deficits averaged 1–2 percent of national income throughout this period). This posed no problem, because their income from foreign assets totaled more than 5 percent of national income. Their balance of payments was thus strongly positive, which enabled them to increase their holdings of foreign assets year after year. In other words, the rest of the world worked to increase consumption by the colonial powers and at the same time became more and more indebted to those same powers. This may seem shocking. But it is essential to realize that the goal of accumulating assets abroad by way of commercial surpluses and colonial appropriations was precisely to be in a position later to run trade deficits. There would be no interest in running trade surpluses forever. The advantage of owning things is that one can continue to consume and accumulate without having to work, or at any rate continue to consume and accumulate more than one could produce on one's own. The same was true on an international scale in the age of colonialism. In the wake of the cumulative shocks of two world wars, the Great Depression, and decolonization, these vast stocks of foreign assets would eventually evaporate. In the 1950s, both France and Great Britain found themselves with net foreign asset holdings close to zero, which means that their foreign assets were just enough to balance the assets of the two former colonial powers owned by the rest of the world. Broadly speaking, this situation did not change much over the next half century. Between 1950 and 2010, the net foreign asset holdings of France and Britain varied from slightly positive to slightly negative while remaining quite close to zero, at least when compared with the levels observed previously. Finally, when we compare the structure of national capital in the eighteenth century to its structure now, we find that net foreign assets play a negligible role in both periods, and that the real long-run structural change is to be found in the gradual replacement of farmland by real estate and working capital, while the total capital stock has remained more or less unchanged relative to national income. Income and Wealth: Some Orders of Magnitude To sum up these changes, it is useful to take today's world as a reference point. The current per capita national income in Britain and France is on the order of 30,000 euros per year, and national capital is about 6 times national income, or roughly 180,000 euros per head. In both countries, farmland is virtually worthless today (a few thousand euros per person at most), and national capital is broadly speaking divided into two nearly equal parts: on average, each citizen has about 90,000 euros in housing (for his or her own use or for rental to others) and about 90,000 euros worth of other domestic capital (primarily in the form of capital invested in firms by way of financial instruments). As a thought experiment, let us go back three centuries and apply the national capital structure as it existed around 1700 but with the average amounts we find today: 30,000 euros annual income per capita and 180,000 euros of capital. Our representative French or British citizen would then own around 120,000 euros worth of land, 30,000 euros worth of housing, and 30,000 euros in other domestic assets. Clearly, some of these people (for example, Jane Austen's characters: John Dashwood with his Norland estate and Charles Darcy with Pemberley) owned hundreds of hectares 6 7 8 —capital worth tens or hundreds of millions of euros—while many others owned nothing at all. But these averages give us a somewhat more concrete idea of the way the structure of national capital has been utterly transformed since the eighteenth century while preserving roughly the same value in terms of annual income. Now imagine this British or French person at the turn of the twentieth century, still with an average income of 30,000 euros and an average capital of 180,000. In Britain, farmland already accounted for only a small fraction of this wealth: 10,000 for each British subject, compared with 50,000 euros worth of housing and 60,000 in other domestic assets, together with nearly 60,000 in foreign investments. France was somewhat similar, except that each citizen still owned on average between 30,000 and 40,000 euros worth of land and roughly the same amount of foreign assets. In both countries, foreign assets had taken on considerable importance. Once again, it goes without saying that not everyone owned shares in the Suez Canal or Russian bonds. But by averaging over the entire population, which contained many people with no foreign assets at all and a small minority with substantial portfolios, we are able to measure the vast quantity of accumulated wealth in the rest of the world that French and British foreign asset holdings represented. Public Wealth, Private Wealth Before studying more precisely the nature of the shocks sustained by capital in the twentieth century and the reasons for the revival of capital since World War II, it will be useful at this point to broach the issue of the public debt, and more generally the division of national capital between public and private assets. Although it is difficult today, in an age where rich countries tend to accumulate substantial public debts, to remember that the public sector balance sheet includes assets as well as liabilities, we should be careful to bear this fact in mind. To be sure, the distinction between public and private capital changes neither the total amount nor the composition of national capital, whose evolution I have just traced. Nevertheless, the division of property rights between the government and private individuals is of considerable political, economic, and social importance. I will begin, then, by recalling the definitions introduced in Chapter 1. National capital (or wealth) is the sum of public capital and private capital. Public capital is the difference between the assets and liabilities of the state (including all public agencies), and private capital is of course the difference between the assets and liabilities of private individuals. Whether public or private, capital is always defined as net wealth, that is, the difference between the market value of what one owns (assets) and what one owes (liabilities, or debts). Concretely, public assets take two forms. They can be nonfinancial (meaning essentially public buildings, used for government offices or for the provision of public services, primarily in health and education: schools, universities, hospitals, etc.) or financial. Governments can own shares in firms, in which they can have a majority or minority stake. These firms may be located within the nation's borders or abroad. In recent years, for instance, so-called sovereign wealth funds have arisen to manage the substantial portfolios of foreign financial assets that some states have acquired. In practice, the boundary between financial and nonfinancial assets need not be fixed. For example, when the French government transformed France Telecom and the French Post Office into 9 shareholder-owned corporations, state-owned buildings used by both firms began to be counted as financial assets of the state, whereas previously they were counted as nonfinancial assets. At present, the total value of public assets (both financial and non-financial) is estimated to be almost one year's national income in Britain and a little less than 1 1/2 times that amount in France. Since the public debt of both countries amounts to about one year's national income, net public wealth (or capital) is close to zero. According to the most recent official estimates by the statistical services and central banks of both countries, Britain's net public capital is almost exactly zero and France's is slightly less than 30 percent of national income (or one-twentieth of total national capital: see Table 3.1). In other words, if the governments of both countries decided to sell off all their assets in order to immediately pay off their debts, nothing would be left in Britain and very little in France. Once again, we should not allow ourselves to be misled by the precision of these estimates. Countries do their best to apply the standardized concepts and methods established by the United Nations and other international organizations, but national accounting is not, and never will be, an exact science. Estimating public debts and financial assets poses no major problems. By contrast, it is not easy to set a precise market value on public buildings (such as schools and hospitals) or transportation infrastructure (such as railway lines and highways) since these are not regularly sold. In theory, such items are priced by observing the sales of similar items in the recent past, but such comparisons are not always reliable, especially since market prices frequently fluctuate, sometimes wildly. Hence these figures should be taken as rough estimates, not mathematical certainties.

In any event, there is absolutely no doubt that net public wealth in both countries is quite small and certainly insignificant compared with total private wealth. Whether net public wealth represents less than 1 percent of national wealth, as in Britain, or about 5 percent, as in France, or even 10 percent if we assume that the value of public assets is seriously underestimated, is ultimately of little or no 10 importance for present purposes. Regardless of the imperfections of measurement, the crucial fact here is that private wealth in 2010 accounts for virtually all of national wealth in both countries: more than 99 percent in Britain and roughly 95 percent in France, according to the latest available estimates. In any case, the true figure is certainly greater than 90 percent.

Public Wealth in Historical Perspective If we examine the history of public wealth in Britain and France since the eighteenth century, as well as the evolution of the public-private division of national capital, we find that the foregoing description has almost always been accurate To a first approximation, public assets and liabilities, and a fortiori the difference between the two, have generally represented very limited amounts compared with the enormous mass of private wealth. In both countries, net public wealth over the past three centuries has sometimes been positive, sometimes negative. But the oscillations, which have ranged, broadly speaking, between +100 and −100 percent of national income (and more often than not between +50 and −50) have all in all been limited in amplitude compared to the high levels of private wealth (as much as 700–800 percent of national income). In other words, the history of the ratio of national capital to national income in France and Britain since the eighteenth century, summarized earlier, has largely been the history of the relation between private capital and national income.

The crucial fact here is of course well known: France and Britain have always been countries based on private property and never experimented with Soviet-style communism, where the state takes control of most capital. Hence it is not surprising that private wealth has always dominated public wealth. Conversely, neither country has ever amassed public debts sufficiently large to radically alter the magnitude of private wealth. With this central fact in mind, it behooves us to push the analysis a bit farther.

Even though public policy never went to extremes in either country, it did have a nonnegligible impact on the accumulation of private wealth at several points, and in different directions. In eighteenth- and nineteenth-century Britain, the government tended at times to increase private wealth by running up large public debts. The French government did the same under the Ancien Régime and in the Belle Époque. At other times, however, the government tried to reduce the magnitude of private wealth. In France after World War II, public debts were canceled, and a large public sector was created; the same was true to a lesser extent in Britain during the same period. At present, both countries (along with most other wealthy countries) are running large public debts. Historical experience shows, however, that this can change fairly rapidly. It will therefore useful to lay some groundwork by studying historical reversals of policy in Britain and France. Both countries offer a rich and varied historical experience in this regard.

I begin with the British case. On two occasions—first at the end of the Napoleonic wars and again after World War II—Britain's public debt attained extremely high levels, around 200 percent of GDP or even slightly above that. Although no country has sustained debt levels as high as Britain's for a longer period of time, Britain never defaulted on its debt. Indeed, the latter fact explains the former: if a country does not default in one way or another, either directly by simply repudiating its debt or indirectly through high inflation, it can take a very long time to pay off such a large public debt. In this respect, Britain's public debt in the nineteenth century is a textbook case. To look back a little farther in time: even before the Revolutionary War in America, Britain had accumulated large public debts in the eighteenth century, as had France. Both monarchies were frequently at war, both with each other and with other European countries, and they did not manage to collect enough in taxes to pay for their expenditures, so that public debt rose steeply. Both countries thus managed to amass debts on the order of 50 percent of national income in the period 1700–1720 and 100 percent of national income in the period 1760–1770. The French monarchy's inability to modernize its tax system and eliminate the fiscal privileges of the nobility is well known, as is the ultimate revolutionary resolution, initiated by the convocation of the Estates General in 1789, that led eventually to the introduction of a new tax system in 1790–1791. A land tax was imposed on all landowners and an estate tax on all inherited wealth. In 1797 came what was called the "banqueroute des deux tiers," or "two-thirds bankruptcy," which was in fact a massive default on two-thirds of the outstanding public debt, compounded by high inflation triggered by the issuance of assignats (paper money backed by nationalized land). This was how the debts of the Ancien Régime were ultimately dealt with. The French public debt was thus quickly reduced to a very low level in the first decades of the nineteenth century (less than 20 percent of national income in 1815). Britain followed a totally different trajectory. In order to finance its war with the American 11 revolutionaries as well as its many wars with France in the revolutionary and Napoleonic eras, the British monarchy chose to borrow without limit. The public debt consequently rose to 100 percent of national income in the early 1770s and to nearly 200 percent in the 1810s—10 times France's debt in the same period. It would take a century of budget surpluses to gradually reduce Britain's debt to under 30 percent of national income in the 1910s

What lessons can we draw from this historical experience? First, there is no doubt that Britain's high level of public debt enhanced the influence of private wealth in British society. Britons who had the necessary means lent what the state demanded without appreciably reducing private investment: the very substantial increase in public debt in the period 1770–1810 was financed largely by a corresponding increase in private saving (proving that the propertied class in Britain was indeed prosperous and that yields on government bonds were attractive), so that national capital remained stable overall at around seven years of national income throughout the period, whereas private wealth rose to more than eight years of national income in the 1810s, as net public capital fell into increasingly negative territory

Hence it is no surprise that wealth is ubiquitous in Jane Austen's novels: traditional landlords were joined by unprecedented numbers of government bondholders. (These were largely the same people, if literary sources count as reliable historical sources.) The result was an exceptionally high level of overall private wealth. Interest on British government bonds supplemented land rents as private capital grew to dimensions never before seen. Second, it is also quite clear that, all things considered, this very high level of public debt served the interests of the lenders and their descendants quite well, at least when compared with what would have happened if the British monarchy had financed its expenditures by making them pay taxes. Fromthe standpoint of people with the means to lend to the government, it is obviously far more advantageous to lend to the state and receive interest on the loan for decades than to pay taxes without compensation.

Furthermore, the fact that the government's deficits increased the overall demand for private wealth inevitably increased the return on that wealth, thereby serving the interests of those whose prosperity depended on the return on their investment in government bonds. The central fact—and the essential difference from the twentieth century—is that the compensation to those who lent to the government was quite high in the nineteenth century: inflation was virtually zero from 1815 to 1914, and the interest rate on government bonds was generally around 4–5 percent; in particular, it was significantly higher than the growth rate. Under such conditions, investing in public debt can be very good business for wealthy people and their heirs. Concretely, imagine a government that runs deficits on the order of 5 percent of GDP every year for twenty years (to pay, say, the wages of a large number of soldiers from 1795 to 1815) without having to increase taxes by an equivalent amount. After twenty years, an additional public debt of 100 percent of GDP will have been accumulated. Suppose that the government does not seek to repay the principal and simply pays the annual interest due on the debt. If the interest rate is 5 percent, it will have to pay 5 percent of GDP every year to the owners of this additional public debt, and must continue to do so until the end of time. In broad outline, this is what Britain did in the nineteenth century. For an entire century, from 1815 to 1914, the British budget was always in substantial primary surplus: in other words, tax revenues always exceeded expenditures by several percent of GDP—an amount greater, for example, than the total expenditure on education throughout this period. It was only the growth of Britain's domestic product and national income (nearly 2.5 percent a year from 1815 to 1914) that ultimately, after a century of penance, allowed the British to significantly reduce their public debt as a percentage of national income. Who Profits from Public Debt? This historical record is fundamental for a number of reasons. First, it enables us to understand why nineteenth-century socialists, beginning with Marx, were so wary of public debt, which they saw—not without a certain perspicacity—as a tool of private capital. This concern was all the greater because in those days investors in public debt were paid handsomely, not only in Britain but also in many other countries, including France. There was no repeat of the revolutionary bankruptcy of 1797, and the rentiers in Balzac's novels do not seem to have worried any more about their government bonds than those in Jane Austen's works. Indeed, inflation was as low in France as in Britain in the period 1815–1914, and interest on government bonds was always paid in a timely manner. French sovereign debt was a good investment throughout the nineteenth century, and private investors prospered on the proceeds, just as in Britain. Although the total outstanding public debt in France was quite limited in 1815, the amount grew over the next several decades, particularly during the Restoration and July Monarchy (1815–1848), during which the right to vote was based on a property qualification. The French government incurred large debts in 1815–1816 to pay for an indemnity to the occupying forces and then again in 1825 to finance the notorious "émigrés' billion," a sum paid to aristocrats who fled France during the Revolution (to compensate them for the rather limited redistribution of land that took place in their absence). Under the Second Empire, financial interests were well served. In the fierce articles that Marx penned in 1849–1850, published in The Class Struggle in France, he took offense at the way Louis-Napoleon Bonaparte's new minister of finance, Achille Fould, representing bankers and financiers, peremptorily decided to increase the tax on drinks in order to pay rentiers their due. Later, after the Franco-Prussian War of 1870–1871, the French government once again had to borrow from its population to pay for a transfer of funds to Germany equivalent to approximately 30 percent of national income. In the end, during the period 1880–1914, the French public debt was even higher than the British: 70 to 80 percent of national income compared with less than 50 percent. In French novels of the Belle Époque, interest on government bonds figured significantly. The government paid roughly 2–3 percent of national income in interest every year (more than the budget for national education), and a very substantial group of people lived on that interest. In the twentieth century, a totally different view of public debt emerged, based on the conviction that debt could serve as an instrument of policy aimed at raising public spending and redistributing wealth for the benefit of the least well-off members of society. The difference between these two views is fairly simple: in the nineteenth century, lenders were handsomely reimbursed, thereby increasing private wealth; in the twentieth century, debt was drowned by inflation and repaid with money of decreasing value. In practice, this allowed deficits to be financed by those who had lent 12 13 14 money to the state, and taxes did not have to be raised by an equivalent amount. This "progressive" view of public debt retains its hold on many minds today, even though inflation has long since declined to a rate not much above the nineteenth century's, and the distributional effects are relatively obscure. It is interesting to recall that redistribution via inflation was much more significant in France than in Britain.

In Britain, things were done differently: more slowly and with less passion. Between 1913 and 1950, the average rate of inflation was a little more than 3 percent a year, which meant that prices increased by a factor of 3 (less than one-thirtieth as much as in France). For British rentiers, this was nevertheless a spoliation of a sort that would have been unimaginable in the nineteenth century, indeed right up to World War I. Still, it was hardly sufficient to prevent an enormous accumulation of public deficits during two world wars: Britain was fully mobilized to pay for the war effort without undue dependence on the printing press, with the result that by 1950 the country found itself saddled with a colossal debt, more than 200 percent of GDP, even higher than in 1815. Only with the inflation of the 1950s (more than 4 percent a year) and above all of the 1970s (nearly 15 percent a year) did Britain's debt fall to around 50 percent of GDP

The mechanism of redistribution via inflation is extremely powerful, and it played a crucial historical role in both Britain and France in the twentieth century. It nevertheless raises two major problems. First, it is relatively crude in its choice of targets: among people with some measure of wealth, those who own government bonds (whether directly or indirectly via bank deposits) are not always the wealthiest: far from it. Second, the inflation mechanism cannot work indefinitely. Once inflation becomes permanent, lenders will demand a higher nominal interest rate, and the higher price will not have the desired effects. Furthermore, high inflation tends to accelerate constantly, and once the process is under way, its consequences can be difficult to master: some social groups saw their incomes rise considerably, while others did not. It was in the late 1970s—a decade marked by a mix of inflation, rising unemployment, and relative economic stagnation ("stagflation")—that a new consensus formed around the idea of low inflation. I will return to this issue later. The Ups and Downs of Ricardian Equivalence This long and tumultuous history of public debt, from the tranquil rentiers of the eighteenth and nineteenth centuries to the expropriation by inflation of the twentieth century, has indelibly marked collective memories and representations. The same historical experiences have also left their mark on economists. For example, when David Ricardo formulated in 1817 the hypothesis known today as "Ricardian equivalence," according to which, under certain conditions, public debt has no effect on the accumulation of national capital, he was obviously strongly influenced by what he witnessed around him. At the moment he wrote, British public debt was close to 200 percent of GDP, yet it seemed not to have dried up the flow of private investment or the accumulation of capital. The much feared "crowding out" phenomenon had not occurred, and the increase in public debt seemed to have been financed by an increase in private saving. To be sure, it does not follow from this that Ricardian equivalence is a universal law, valid in all times and places. Everything of course depended on the prosperity of the social group involved (in Ricardo's day, a minority of Britons with enough wealth to generate the additional savings required), on the rate of interest that was offered, and of course on confidence in the government. But it is a fact worth noting that Ricardo, who had no access to historical time series or measurements of the type indicated i n Figure 3.3 but who had intimate knowledge of the British capitalism of his time, clearly recognized that Britain's gigantic public debt had no apparent impact on national wealth and simply constituted a claim of one portion of the population on another. Similarly, when John Maynard Keynes wrote in 1936 about "the euthanasia of the rentier," he was also deeply impressed by what he observed around him: the pre–World War I world of the rentier was collapsing, and there was in fact no other politically acceptable way out of the economic and budgetary crisis of the day. In particular, Keynes clearly felt that inflation, which the British were still reluctant to accept because of strong conservative attachment to the pre-1914 gold standard, would be the simplest though not necessarily the most just way to reduce the burden of public debt and the influence of accumulated wealth. Since the 1970s, analyses of the public debt have suffered from the fact that economists have probably relied too much on so-called representative agent models, that is, models in which each agent is assumed to earn the same income and to be endowed with the same amount of wealth (and thus to own the same quantity of government bonds). Such a simplification of reality can be useful at times in order to isolate logical relations that are difficult to analyze in more complex models. Yet by totally avoiding the issue of inequality in the distribution of wealth and income, these models often lead to extreme and unrealistic conclusions and are therefore a source of confusion rather than clarity. In the case of public debt, representative agent models can lead to the conclusion that government debt is completely neutral, in regard not only to the total amount of national capital but also to the distribution of the fiscal burden. This radical reinterpretation of Ricardian equivalence, which was first proposed by the American economist Robert Barro, fails to take account of the fact that the bulk of the public debt is in practice owned by a minority of the population (as in nineteenth-century Britain but not only there), so that the debt is the vehicle of important internal redistributions when it is repaid as well as when it is not. In view of the high degree of concentration that has always been characteristic of the wealth distribution, to study these questions without asking about inequalities between social groups is in fact to say nothing about significant aspects of the subject and what is 15 16 really at stake. France: A Capitalism without Capitalists in the Postwar Period I return now to the history of public wealth and to the question of assets held by the government. Compared with the history of government debt, the history of public assets is seemingly less tumultuous. To simplify, one can say that the total value of public assets increased over the long run in both France and Britain, rising from barely 50 percent of national income in the eighteenth and nineteenth centuries to roughly 100 percent at the end of the twentieth century (see Figures 3.3 and 3.4). To a first approximation, this increase reflects the steady expansion of the economic role of the state over the course of history, including in particular the development of ever more extensive public services in the areas of health and education (necessitating major investments in buildings and equipment) together with public or semipublic infrastructural investments in transportation and communication. These public services and infrastructures are more extensive in France than in Britain: the total value of public assets in France in 2010 is close to 150 percent of national income, compared with barely 100 percent across the Channel. Nevertheless, this simplified, tranquil view of the accumulation of public assets over the long run omits an important aspect of the history of the last century: the accumulation of significant public assets in the industrial and financial sectors in the period 1950–1980, followed by major waves of privatization of the same assets after 1980. Both phenomena can be observed to varying degrees in most developed countries, especially in Europe, as well as in many emerging economies. The case of France is emblematic. To understand it, we can look back in time. Not only in France but in countries around the world, faith in private capitalism was greatly shaken by the economic crisis of the 1930s and the cataclysms that followed. The Great Depression, triggered by the Wall Street crash of October 1929, struck the wealthy countries with a violence that has never been repeated to this day: a quarter of the working population in the United States, Germany, Britain, and France found themselves out of work. The traditional doctrine of "laissez faire," or nonintervention by the state in the economy, to which all countries adhered in the nineteenth century and to a large extent until the early 1930s, was durably discredited. Many countries opted for a greater degree of interventionism. Naturally enough, governments and the general public questioned the wisdom of financial and economic elites who had enriched themselves while leading the world to disaster. People began to think about different types of "mixed" economy, involving varying degrees of public ownership of firms alongside traditional forms of private property, or else, at the very least, a strong dose of public regulation and supervision of the financial system and of private capitalism more generally. Furthermore, the fact that the Soviet Union joined the victorious Allies in World War II enhanced the prestige of the statist economic system the Bolsheviks had put in place. Had not that systemallowed the Soviets to lead a notoriously backward country, which in 1917 had only just emerged from serfdom, on a forced march to industrialization? In 1942, Joseph Schumpeter believed that socialism would inevitably triumph over capitalism. In 1970, when Paul Samuelson published the eighth edition of his famous textbook, he was still predicting that the GDP of the Soviet Union might 17 outstrip that of the United States sometime between 1990 and 2000. In France, this general climate of distrust toward private capitalism was deepened after 1945 by the fact that many members of the economic elite were suspected of having collaborated with the German occupiers and indecently enriched themselves during the war. It was in this highly charged post-Liberation climate that major sectors of the economy were nationalized, including in particular the banking sector, the coal mines, and the automobile industry. The Renault factories were punitively seized after their owner, Louis Renault, was arrested as a collaborator in September 1944. The provisional government nationalized the firm in January 1945. In 1950, according to available estimates, the total value of French public assets exceeded one year's national income. Since the value of public debt had been sharply reduced by inflation, net public wealth was close to one year's national income, at a time when total private wealth was worth barely two years of national income (see Figure 3.6). As usual, one should not be misled by the apparent precision of these estimates: it is difficult to measure the value of capital in this period, when asset prices had attained historic lows, and it is possible that public assets are slightly undervalued compared with private assets. But the orders of magnitude may be taken as significant: in 1950, the government of France owned 25–30 percent of the nation's wealth, and perhaps even a little more.

This is a significant proportion, especially in view of the fact that public ownership left small and medium firms untouched, along with agriculture, and never claimed more than a minority share (less than 20 percent) of residential real estate. In the industrial and financial sectors most directly affected by the postwar nationalizations, the state's share of national wealth exceeded 50 percent from 1950 to 1980. Although this historical episode was relatively brief, it is important for understanding the complex attitude of the French people toward private capitalism even today. Throughout the Trente Glorieuses, during which the country was rebuilt and economic growth was strong (stronger that at any other time in the nation's history), France had a mixed economy, in a sense a capitalism without capitalists, or at any rate a state capitalism in which private owners no longer controlled the largest firms. To be sure, waves of nationalization also occurred in this same period in many other countries, including Britain, where the value of public assets also exceeded a year's national income in 1950—a level equal to that of France. The difference is that British public debt at the time exceeded two years of national income, so that net public wealth was significantly negative in the 1950s, and private wealth was that much greater. Net public wealth did not turn positive in Britain until the 1960s–1970s, and even then it remained less than 20 percent of national income (which is already quite large). What is distinctive about the French trajectory is that public ownership, having thrived from 1950 to 1980, dropped to very low levels after 1980, even as private wealth—both financial and real estate—rose to levels even higher than Britain's: nearly six years of national income in 2010, or 20 times the value of public wealth. Following a period of state capitalism after 1950, France became the promised land of the new private-ownership capitalism of the twenty-first century. What makes the change all the more striking is that it was never clearly acknowledged for what it was. The privatization of the economy, including both liberalization of the market for goods and 17 18 19 services and deregulation of financial markets and capital flows, which affected countries around theworld in the 1980s, had multiple and complex origins. The memory of the Great Depression andsubsequent disasters had faded. The "stagflation" of the 1970s demonstrated the limits of the postwarKeynesian consensus. With the end of postwar reconstruction and the high growth rates of the TrenteGlorieuses, it was only natural to question the wisdom of indefinitely expanding the role of the stateand its increasing claims on national output. The deregulation movement began with the "conservativerevolutions" of 1979–1980 in the United States and Britain, as both countries increasingly chafed atbeing overtaken by others (even though the catch-up was a largely inevitable process, as noted inChapter 2). Meanwhile, the increasingly obvious failure of statist Soviet and Chinese models in the1970s led both communist giants to begin a gradual liberalization of their economic systems in the1980s by introducing new forms of private property in firms. Despite these converging international currents, French voters in 1981 displayed a certain desire tosail against the wind. Every country has its own history, of course, and its own political timetable. InFrance, a coalition of Socialists and Communists won a majority on a platform that promised tocontinue the nationalization of the industrial and banking sectors begun in 1945. This proved to be abrief intermezzo, however, since in 1986 a liberal majority initiated a very important wave ofprivatization in all sectors. This initiative was then continued and amplified by a new socialistmajority in the period 1988–1993. The Renault Company became a joint-stock corporation in 1990,as did the public telecommunications administration, which was transformed into France Telecomand opened to private investment in 1997–1998. In a context of slower growth, high unemployment,and large government deficits, the progressive sale of publicly held shares after 1990 broughtadditional funds into public coffers, although it did not prevent a steady increase in the public debt.Net public wealth fell to very low levels. Meanwhile, private wealth slowly returned to levels notseen since the shocks of the twentieth century. In this way, France totally transformed its nationalcapital structure at two different points in time without really understanding why.

CHAPTER FOUR

From Old Europe to the New World

The lessons to be learned from each country proved consistent and complementary. The nature of capital was totally transformed, but in the end its total amount relative to income scarcely changed at all. To gain a better understanding of the different historical processes and mechanisms involved, the analysis must now extend to other countries. I will begin by looking at Germany, which will round out the European panorama. Then I will turn my attention to capital in North America (the United States and Canada). Capital in the New World took some quite unusual and specific forms, in the first place because land was so abundant that it did not cost very much; second, because of the existence of slavery; and finally, because this region of perpetual demographic growth tended to accumulate structurally smaller amounts of capital (relative to annual income and output) than Europe did. This will lead to the question of what fundamentally determines the capital/income ratio in the long run, which will be the subject of Chapter 5. I will approach that question by extending the analysis first to all the wealthy countries and then to the entire globe, insofar as the sources allow

Germany: Rhenish Capitalism and Social Ownership I begin with the case of Germany. It is interesting to compare the British and French trajectories with the German, especially in regard to the issue of mixed economy, which became important, as noted, after World War II. Unfortunately, the historical data for Germany are more diverse, owing to the lateness of German unification and numerous territorial changes, so there is no satisfactory way to trace the history back beyond 1870. Still, the estimates we have for the period after 1870 reveal clear similarities with Britain and France, as well as a number of differences.

The first thing to notice is that the overall evolution is similar: first, agricultural land gave way in the long run to residential and commercial real estate and industrial and financial capital, and second, the capital/income ratio has grown steadily since World War II and appears to be on its way to regaining the level it had attained prior to the shocks of 1914–1945

Note that the importance of farmland in late nineteenth-century Germany made the German case resemble the French more than the British one (agriculture had not yet disappeared east of the Rhine), and the value of industrial capital was higher than in either France or Britain. By contrast, Germany on the eve of World War I had only half as much in foreign assets as France (roughly 50 percent of national income versus a year's worth of income for France) and only a quarter as much as Britain (whose foreign assets were worth two years of national income). The main reason for this is of course that Germany had no colonial empire, a fact that was the source of some very powerful political and military tensions: think, for example, of the Moroccan crises of 1905 and 1911, when the Kaiser sought to challenge French supremacy in Morocco. The heightened competition among European powers for colonial assets obviously contributed to the climate that ultimately led to the declaration of war in the summer of 1914: one need not subscribe to all of Lenin's theses in Imperialism, the Highest Stage of Capitalism (1916) to share this conclusion. Note, too, that Germany over the past several decades has amassed substantial foreign assets thanks to trade surpluses. By 2010, Germany's net foreign asset position was close to 50 percent of national income (more than half of which has been accumulated since 2000). This is almost the same level as in 1913. It is a small amount compared to the foreign asset positions of Britain and France at the end of the nineteenth century, but it is substantial compared to the current positions of the two former colonial powers, which are close to zero.

different the trajectories of Germany, France, and Britain have been since the nineteenth century: to a certain extent they have inverted their respective positions. In view of Germany's very large current trade surpluses, it is not impossible that this divergence will increase. I will come back to this point. In regard to public debt and the split between public and private capital, the German trajectory is fairly similar to the French. With average inflation of nearly 17 percent between 1930 and 1950, which means that prices were multiplied by a factor of 300 between those dates (compared with barely 100 in France), Germany was the country that, more than any other, drowned its public debt in inflation in the twentieth century. Despite running large deficits during both world wars (the public debt briefly exceeded 100 percent of GDP in 1918–1920 and 150 percent of GDP in 1943–1944), inflation made it possible in both instances to shrink the debt very rapidly to very low levels: barely 20 percent of GDP in 1930 and again in 1950.

There is, however, a significant difference between the value of private capital in Germany compared to that in France and Britain. German private wealth has increased enormously since World War II: it was exceptionally low in 1950 (barely a year and a half of national income), but today it stands at more than four years of national income. The reconstitution of private wealth in all three countries emerges clearlyNevertheless, German private wealth in 2010 was noticeably lower than private wealth in Britain and France: barely four years of national income in Germany compared with five or six in France and Britain and more than six in Italy and Spain

Given the high level of German saving, this low level of German wealth compared to other European countries is to some extent a paradox, which may be transitory and can be explained as follows. The first factor to consider is the low price of real estate in Germany compared to other European countries, which can be explained in part by the fact that the sharp price increases seen everywhere else after 1990 were checked in Germany by the effects of German reunification, which brought a large number of low-cost houses onto the market. To explain the discrepancy over the long term, however, we would need more durable factors, such as stricter rent control.

In any case, most of the gap between Germany on the one hand and France and Britain on the other stems not from the difference in the value of the housing stock but rather from the difference in the value of other domestic capital, and primarily the capital of firms In other words, the gap arises not from the low valuation of German real estate but rather from the low stock market valuation of German firms. If, in measuring total private wealth, we used not stock market value but book value (obtained by subtracting a firm's debt from the cumulative value of its investments), the German paradox would disappear: German private wealth would immediately rise to French and British levels (between five and six years of national income rather than four). These complications may appear to be purely matters of accounting but are in fact highly political. At this stage, suffice it to say that the lower market values of German firms appear to reflect the character of what is sometimes called "Rhenish capitalism" or "the stakeholder model," that is, an economic model in which firms are owned not only by shareholders but also by certain other interested parties known as "stakeholders," starting with representatives of the firms' workers (who 4 sit on the boards of directors of German firms not merely in a consultative capacity but as active participants in deliberations, even though they may not be shareholders), as well as representatives of regional governments, consumers' associations, environmental groups, and so on. The point here is not to idealize this model of shared social ownership, which has its limits, but simply to note that it can be at least as efficient economically as Anglo-Saxon market capitalism or "the shareholder model" (in which all power lies in theory with shareholders, although in practice things are always more complex), and especially to observe that the stakeholder model inevitably implies a lower market valuation but not necessarily a lower social valuation. The debate about different varieties of capitalism erupted in the early 1990s after the collapse of the Soviet Union. Its intensity later waned, in part no doubt because the German economic model seemed to be losing steam in the years after reunification (between 1998 and 2002, Germany was often presented as the sick man of Europe). In view of Germany's relatively good health in the midst of the global financial crisis (2007–2012), it is not out of the question that this debate will be revived in the years to come. Shocks to Capital in the Twentieth Century Now that I have presented a first look at the general evolution of the capital/income ratio and the public-private split over the long run, I must return to the question of chronology and in particular attempt to understand the reasons first for the collapse of the capital/income ratio over the course of the twentieth century and then for its spectacular recovery. Note first of all that this was a phenomenon that affected all European countries. All available sources indicate that the changes observed in Britain, France, and Germany (which together in 1910 and again in 2010 account for more than two-thirds of the GDP of Western Europe and more than half of the GDP of all of Europe) are representative of the entire continent: although interesting variations between countries do exist, the overall pattern is the same. In particular, the capital/income ratio in Italy and Spain has risen quite sharply since 1970, even more sharply than in Britain and France, and the available historical data suggest that it was on the order of six or seven years of national income around the turn of the twentieth century. Available estimates for Belgium, the Netherlands, and Austria indicate a similar pattern. Next, we must insist on the fact that the fall in the capital/ income ratio between 1914 and 1945 is explained to only a limited extent by the physical destruction of capital (buildings, factories, infrastructure, etc.) due to the two world wars. In Britain, France, and Germany, the value of national capital was between six and a half and seven years of national income in 1913 and fell to around two and a half years in 1950: a spectacular drop of more than four years of national income . To be sure, there was substantial physical destruction of capital, especially in France during World War I (during which the northeastern part of the country, on the front lines, was severely battered) and in both France and Germany during World War II owing to massive bombing in 1944– 1945 (although the periods of combat were shorter than in World War I, the technology was considerably more destructive). All in all, capital worth nearly a year of national income was destroyed in France (accounting for one-fifth to one-quarter of the total decline in the capital/income ratio), and a year and a half in Germany (or roughly a third of the total decline). Although these losses were quite significant, they clearly explain only a fraction of the total drop, even in the two countries 5 6 7 most directly affected by the conflicts. In Britain, physical destruction was less extensive—insignificant in World War I and less than 10 percent of national income owing to German bombing in World War II—yet national capital fell by four years of national income (or more than 40 times the loss due to physical destruction), as much as in France and Germany.

In fact, the budgetary and political shocks of two wars proved far more destructive to capital than combat itself. In addition to physical destruction, the main factors that explain the dizzying fall in the capital/income ratio between 1913 and 1950 were on the one hand the collapse of foreign portfolios and the very low savings rate characteristic of the time (together, these two factors, plus physical destruction, explain two-thirds to three-quarters of the drop) and on the other the low asset prices that obtained in the new postwar political context of mixed ownership and regulation (which accounted for one-quarter to one-third of the drop). I have already mentioned the importance of losses on foreign assets, especially in Britain, where net foreign capital dropped from two years of national income on the eve of World War I to a slightly negative level in the 1950s. Britain's losses on its international portfolio were thus considerably greater than French or German losses through physical destruction of domestic capital, and these more than made up for the relatively low level of physical destruction on British soil. The decline of foreign capital stemmed in part from expropriations due to revolution and the process of decolonization (think of the Russian loans to which many French savers subscribed in the Belle Époque and that the Bolsheviks repudiated in 1917, or the nationalization of the Suez Canal by Nasser in 1956, to the dismay of the British and French shareholders who owned the canal and had been collecting dividends and royalties on it since 1869) and in even greater part to the very low savings rate observed in various European countries between 1914 and 1945, which led British and French (and to a lesser degree German) savers to gradually sell off their foreign assets. Owing to low growth and repeated recessions, the period 1914–1945 was a dark one for all Europeans but especially for the wealthy, whose income dwindled considerably in comparison with the Belle Époque. Private savings rates were therefore relatively low (especially if we deduct the amount of reparations and replacement of war-damaged property), and some people consequently chose to maintain their standard of living by gradually selling off part of their capital. When the Depression came in the 1930s, moreover, many stock- and bondholders were ruined as firm after firm went bankrupt. Furthermore, the limited amount of private saving was largely absorbed by enormous public deficits, especially during the wars: national saving, the sum of private and public saving, was extremely low in Britain, France, and Germany between 1914 and 1945. Savers lent massively to their governments, in some cases selling their foreign assets, only to be ultimately expropriated by inflation, very quickly in France and Germany and more slowly in Britain, which created the illusion that private wealth in Britain was faring better in 1950 than private wealth on the continent. In fact, national wealth was equally affected in both places.

At times governments borrowed directly from abroad: that is how the United States went from a negative position on the eve of World War I to a positive position in the 1950s. But the effect on the national wealth of Britain or France was the same. Ultimately, the decline in the capital/income ratio between 1913 and 1950 is the history of Europe's suicide, and in particular of the euthanasia of European capitalists. This political, military, and budgetary history would be woefully incomplete, however, if we did not insist on the fact that the low level of the capital/income ratio after World War II was in some ways a positive thing, in that it reflected in part a deliberate policy choice aimed at reducing—more or less consciously and more or less efficaciously—the market value of assets and the economic power of their owners. Concretely, real estate values and stocks fell to historically low levels in the 1950s and 1960s relative to the price of goods and services, and this goes some way toward explaining the low capital/income ratio. Remember that all forms of wealth are evaluated in terms of market prices at a given point in time. This introduces an element of arbitrariness (markets are often capricious), but it is the only method we have for calculating the national capital stock: how else could one possibly add up hectares of farmland, square meters of real estate, and blast furnaces? In the postwar period, housing prices stood at historic lows, owing primarily to rent control policies that were adopted nearly everywhere in periods of high inflation such as the early 1920s and especially the 1940s. Rents rose less sharply than other prices. Housing became less expensive for tenants, while landlords earned less on their properties, so real estate prices fell. Similarly, the value of firms, that is, the value of the stock of listed firms and shares of partnerships, fell to relatively low levels in the 1950s and 1960s. Not only had confidence in the stock markets been strongly shaken by the Depression and the nationalizations of the postwar period, but new policies of financial regulation and taxation of dividends and profits had been established, helping to reduce the power of stockholders and the value of their shares. Detailed estimates for Britain, France, and Germany show that low real estate and stock prices after World War II account for a nonnegligible but still minority share of the fall in the capital/income ratio between 1913 and 1950: between one-quarter and one-third of the drop depending on the country, whereas volume effects (low national savings rate, loss of foreign assets, destructions) account for two-thirds to three-quarters of the decline. Similarly, as I will show in the next chapter, the very strong rebound of real estate and stock market prices in the 1970s and 1980s and especially the 1990s and 2000s explains a significant part of the rebound in the capital/income ratio, though still less important than volume effects, linked this time to a structural decrease in the rate of growth. 8 9 Capital in America: More Stable Than in Europe Before studying in greater detail the rebound in the capital/income ratio in the second half of the twentieth century and analyzing the prospects for the twenty-first century, I now want to move beyond the European framework to examine the historical forms and levels of capital in America. Several facts stand out clearly. First, America was the New World, where capital mattered less than in the Old World, meaning old Europe. More precisely, the value of the stock of national capital, based on numerous contemporary estimates I have collected and compared, as for other countries, was scarcely more than three years of national income around the time that the United States gained its independence, in the period 1770–1810. Farmland was valued at between one and one and a half years of national income.

Uncertainties notwithstanding, there is no doubt that the capital/income ratio was much lower in the New World colonies than in Britain or France, where national capital was worth roughly seven years of national income, of which farmland accounted for nearly four.

The crucial point is that the number of hectares per person was obviously far greater in North America than in old Europe. In volume, capital per capita was therefore higher in the United States. Indeed, there was so much land that its market value was very low: anyone could own vast quantities, and therefore it was not worth very much. In other words, the price effect more than counterbalanced the volume effect: when the volume of a given type of capital exceeds certain thresholds, its price will inevitably fall to a level so low that the product of the price and volume, which is the value of the capital, is lower than it would be if the volume were smaller.

The considerable difference between the price of land in the New World and in Europe at the end of the eighteenth century and the beginning of the nineteenth is confirmed by all available sources concerning land purchases and inheritances (such as probate records and wills). Furthermore, the other types of capital—housing and other domestic capital—were also relatively less important in the colonial era and during the early years of the American republic (in comparison to Europe). The reason for this is different, but the fact is not surprising. New arrivals, who accounted for a very large proportion of the US population, did not cross the Atlantic with their capital of homes or tools or machinery, and it took time to accumulate the equivalent of several years of national income in real estate and business capital. Make no mistake: the low capital/income ratio in America reflected a fundamental difference in the structure of social inequalities compared with Europe. The fact that total wealth amounted to barely three years of national income in the United States compared with more than seven in Europe signified in a very concrete way that the influence of landlords and accumulated wealth was less important in the New World. With a few years of work, the new arrivals were able to close the initial gap between themselves and their wealthier predecessors—or at any rate it was possible to close the wealth gap more rapidly than in Europe. In 1840, Tocqueville noted quite accurately that "the number of large fortunes [in the United

States] is quite small, and capital is still scarce," and he saw this as one obvious reason for the democratic spirit that in his view dominated there. He added that, as his observations showed, all of this was a consequence of the low price of agricultural land: "In America, land costs little, and anyone can easily become a landowner." Here we can see at work the Jeffersonian ideal of a society of small landowners, free and equal. Things would change over the course of the nineteenth century. The share of agriculture in output decreased steadily, and the value of farmland also declined, as in Europe. But the United States accumulated a considerable stock of real estate and industrial capital, so that national capital was close to five years of national income in 1910, versus three in 1810. The gap with old Europe remained, but it had shrunk by half in one century .The United States had become capitalist, but wealth continued to have less influence than in Belle Époque Europe, at least if we consider the vast US territory as a whole. If we limit our gaze to the East Coast, the gap is smaller still. In the film Titanic, the director, James Cameron, depicted the social structure of 1912. He chose to make wealthy Americans appear just as prosperous—and arrogant—as their European counterparts: for instance, the detestable Hockley, who wants to bring young Rose to Philadelphia in order to marry her. (Heroically, she refuses to be treated as property and becomes Rose Dawson.) The novels of Henry James that are set in Boston and New York between 1880 and 1910 also show social groups in which real estate and industrial and financial capital matter almost as much as in European novels: times had indeed changed since the Revolutionary War, when the United States was still a land without capital. The shocks of the twentieth century struck America with far less violence than Europe, so that the capital/income ratio remained far more stable: it oscillated between four and five years of national income from 1910 to 2010.

To be sure, US fortunes were also buffeted by the crises of 1914–1945. Public debt rose sharply in the United States due to the cost of waging war, especially during World War II, and this affected national saving in a period of economic instability: the euphoria of the 1920s gave way to the Depression of the 1930s. (Cameron tells us that the odious Hockley commits suicide in October 1929.). Under Franklin D. Roosevelt, moreover, the United States adopted policies designed to reduce the influence of private capital, such as rent control, just as in Europe. After World War II, real estate and stock prices stood at historic lows. When it came to progressive taxation, the United States went much farther than Europe, possibly demonstrating that the goal there was more to reduce inequality than to eradicate private property. No sweeping policy of nationalization was attempted, although major public investments were initiated in the 1930s and 1940s, especially in infrastructures. Inflation and growth eventually returned public debt to a modest level in the 1950s and 1960s, so that public wealth was distinctly positive in 1970 (see Figure 4.7). In the end, American private wealth decreased from nearly five years of national income in 1930 to less than three and a half in 1970, a not insignificant decline.

Nevertheless, the "U-shaped curve" of the capital/income ratio in the twentieth century is smaller in amplitude in the United States than in Europe. Expressed in years of income or output, capital in the United States seems to have achieved virtual stability from the turn of the twentieth century on—so much so that a stable capital/income or capital/output ratio is sometimes treated as a universal law in US textbooks (like Paul Samuelson's). In comparison, Europe's relation to capital, and especially private capital, was notably chaotic in the century just past. In the Belle Époque capital was king. In the years after World War II many people thought capitalism had been almost eradicated. Yet at the beginning of the twenty-first century Europe seems to be in the avant-garde of the new patrimonial capitalism, with private fortunes once again surpassing US levels. This is fairly well explained by the lower rate of economic and especially demographic growth in Europe compared with the United States, leading automatically to increased influence of wealth accumulated in the past.

The New World and Foreign Capital Another key difference between the history of capital in America and Europe is that foreign capital never had more than a relatively limited importance in the United States. This is because the United States, the first colonized territory to have achieved independence, never became a colonial power itself. Throughout the nineteenth century, the United States' net foreign capital position was slightly negative: what US citizens owned in the rest of the world was less than what foreigners, mainly British, owned in the United States. The difference was quite small, however, at most 10–20 percent of the US national income, and generally less than 10 percent between 1770 and 1920. For example, on the eve of World War I, US domestic capital—farmland, housing, other domestic capital—stood at 500 percent of national income. Of this total, the assets owned by foreign investors (minus foreign assets held by US investors) represented the equivalent of 10 percent of national income. The national capital, or net national wealth, of the United States was thus about 490 percent of national income. In other words, the United States was 98 percent US-owned and 2 percent foreign-owned. The net foreign asset position was close to balanced, especially when compared to the enormous foreign assets held by Europeans: between one and two years of national income in France and Britain and half a year in Germany. Since the GDP of the United States was barely more than half of the GDP of Western Europe in 1913, this also means that the Europeans of 1913 held only a small proportion of their foreign asset portfolios (less than 5 percent) in the United States. To sum up, the world of 1913 was one in which Europe owned a large part of Africa, Asia, and Latin America, while the United States owned itself. With the two world wars, the net foreign asset position of the United States reversed itself: it was negative in 1913 but turned slightly positive in the 1920s and remained so into the 1970s and 1980s. The United States financed the belligerents and thus ceased to be a debtor of Europe and became a creditor. It bears emphasizing, however, that the United States' net foreign assets holdings remained relatively modest: barely 10 percent of national income

In the 1950s and 1960s in particular, the net foreign capital held by the United States was still fairly limited (barely 5 percent of national income, whereas domestic capital was close to 400 percent, or 80 times greater). The investments of US multinational corporations in Europe and the rest of the world attained levels that seemed considerable at the time, especially to Europeans, who were accustomed to owning the world and who chafed at the idea of owing their reconstruction in part to Uncle Sam and the Marshall Plan. In fact, despite these national traumas, US investments in Europe would always be fairly limited compared to the investments the former colonial powers had held around the globe a few decades earlier. Furthermore, US investments in Europe and elsewhere were balanced by continued strong foreign investment in the United States, particularly by Britain. In the series Mad Men, which is set in the early 1960s, the New York advertising agency Sterling Cooper is bought out by distinguished British stockholders, which does not fail to cause a culture shock in the small world of Madison Avenue advertising: it is never easy to be owned by foreigners. The net foreign capital position of the United States turned slightly negative in the 1980s and then increasingly negative in the 1990s and 2000s as a result of accumulating trade deficits. Nevertheless, US investments abroad continued to yield a far better return than the nation paid on its foreign-held debt—such is the privilege due to confidence in the dollar. This made it possible to limit the degradation of the negative US position, which amounted to roughly 10 percent of national income in the 1990s and slightly more than 20 percent in the early 2010s. All in all, the current situation is therefore fairly close to what obtained on the eve of World War I. The domestic capital of the United States is worth about 450 percent of national income. Of this total, assets held by foreign investors (minus foreign assets held by US investors) represent the equivalent of 20 percent of national income. The net national wealth of the United States is therefore about 430 percent of national income. In other words, the United States is more than 95 percent American owned and less than 5 percent foreign owned. To sum up, the net foreign asset position of the United States has at times been slightly negative, at other times slightly positive, but these positions were always of relatively limited importance compared with the total stock of capital owned by US citizens (always less than 5 percent and generally less than 2 percent).

It is interesting to observe that things took a very different course in Canada, where a very significant share of domestic capital—as much as a quarter in the late nineteenth and early twentieth century—was owned by foreign investors, mainly British, especially in the natural resources sector (copper, zinc, and aluminum mines as well as hydrocarbons). In 1910, Canada's domestic capital was valued at 530 percent of national income. Of this total, assets owned by foreign investors (less foreign assets owned by Canadian investors) represented the equivalent of 120 percent of national income, somewhere between one-fifth and one-quarter of the total. Canada's net national wealth was thus equal to about 410 percent of national income

Two world wars changed this situation considerably, as Europeans were forced to sell many foreign assets. This took time, however: from 1950 to 1990, Canada's net foreign debt represented roughly 10 percent of its domestic capital. Public debt rose toward the end of the period before being consolidated after 1990. Today, Canada's situation is fairly close to that of the United States. Its domestic capital is worth roughly 410 percent of its national income. Of this total, assets owned by foreign investors (less foreign assets own by Canadian investors) represent less than 10 percent of national income. Canada is thus more than 98 percent Canadian owned and less than 2 percent foreign owned. (Note, however, that this view of net foreign capital masks the magnitude of cross-ownership between countries, about which I will say more in the next chapter.) This comparison of the United States with Canada is interesting, because it is difficult to find purely economic reasons why these two North American trajectories should differ so profoundly. Clearly, political factors played a central role. Although the United States has always been quite open to foreign investment, it is fairly difficult to imagine that nineteenth-century US citizens would have tolerated a situation in which one-quarter of the country was owned by its former colonizer. This posed less of a problem in Canada, which remained a British colony: the fact that a large part of the country was owned by Britain was therefore not so different from the fact that Londoners owned much of the land and many of the factories in Scotland or Sussex. Similarly, the fact that Canada's net foreign assets remained negative for so long is linked to the absence of any violent political rupture (Canada gradually gained independence from Britain, but its head of state remained the British monarch) and hence to the absence of expropriations of the kind that elsewhere in the world generally accompanied access to independence, especially in regard to natural resources. New World and Old World: The Importance of Slavery I cannot conclude this examination of the metamorphoses of capital in Europe and the United States without examining the issue of slavery and the place of slaves in US fortunes. Thomas Jefferson owned more than just land. He also owned more than six hundred slaves, mostly inherited from his father and father-in-law, and his political attitude toward the slavery question was always extremely ambiguous. His ideal republic of small landowners enjoying equal rights did not include people of color, on whose forced labor the economy of his native Virginia largely depended. 11 12 13 After becoming president of the United States in 1801 thanks to the votes of the southern states, he nevertheless signed a law ending the import of new slaves to US soil after 1808. This did not prevent a sharp increase in the number of slaves (natural increase was less costly than buying new slaves), which rose from around 400,000 in the 1770s to 1 million in the 1800 census. The number more than quadrupled again between 1800 and the census of 1860, which counted more than 4 million slaves: in other words, the number of slaves had increased tenfold in less than a century. The slave economy was growing rapidly when the Civil War broke out in 1861, leading ultimately to the abolition of slavery in 1865. In 1800, slaves represented nearly 20 percent of the population of the United States: roughly 1 million slaves out of a total population of 5 million. In the South, where nearly all of the slaves were held, the proportion reached 40 percent: 1 million slaves and 1.5 million whites for a total population of 2.5 million. Not all whites owned slaves, and only a tiny minority owned as many as Jefferson: fortunes based on slavery were among the most concentrated of all. By 1860, the proportion of slaves in the overall population of the United States had fallen to around 15 percent (about 4 million slaves in a total population of 30 million), owing to rapid population growth in the North and West. In the South, however, the proportion remained at 40 percent: 4 million slaves and 6 million whites for a total population of 10 million. We can draw on any number of historical sources to learn about the price of slaves in the United States between 1770 and 1865. These include probate records assembled by Alice Hanson Jones, tax and census data used by Raymond Goldsmith, and data on slave market transactions collected primarily by Robert Fogel.

What one finds is that the total market value of slaves represented nearly a year and a half of US national income in the late eighteenth century and the first half of the nineteenth century, which is roughly equal to the total value of farmland. If we include slaves along with other components of wealth, we find that total American wealth has remained relatively stable from the colonial era to the present, at around four and a half years of national income .To add the value of slaves to capital in this way is obviously a dubious thing to do in more ways than one: it is the mark of a civilization in which some people were treated as chattel rather than as individuals endowed with rights, including in particular the right to own property. But it does allow us to measure the importance of slave capital for slave owners.

This emerges even more clearly when we distinguish southern from northern states and compare the capital structure in the two regions (slaves included) in the period 1770–1810 with the capital structure in Britain and France in the same period In the American South, the total value of slaves ranged between two and a half and three years of national income, so that the combined value of farmland and slaves exceeded four years of national income. All told, southern slave owners in the New World controlled more wealth than the landlords of old Europe. Their farmland was not worth very much, but since they had the bright idea of owning not just the land but also the labor force needed to work that land, their total capital was even greater. If one adds the market value of slaves to other components of wealth, the value of southern capital exceeds six years of the southern states' income, or nearly as much as the total value of capital in Britain and

France. Conversely, in the North, where there were virtually no slaves, total wealth was indeed quite small: barely three years of the northern states' income, half as much as in the south or Europe.

Clearly, the antebellum United States was far from the country without capital discussed earlier. In fact, the New World combined two diametrically opposed realities. In the North we find a relatively egalitarian society in which capital was indeed not worth very much, because land was so abundant that anyone could became a landowner relatively cheaply, and also because recent immigrants had not had time to accumulate much capital. In the South we find a world where inequalities of ownership took the most extreme and violent form possible, since one half of the population owned the other half: here, slave capital largely supplanted and surpassed landed capital. This complex and contradictory relation to inequality largely persists in the United States to this day: on the one hand this is a country of egalitarian promise, a land of opportunity for millions of immigrants of modest background; on the other it is a land of extremely brutal inequality, especially in relation to race, whose effects are still quite visible. (Southern blacks were deprived of civil rights until the 1960s and subjected to a regime of legal segregation that shared some features in common with the system of apartheid that was maintained in South Africa until the 1980s.) This no doubt accounts for many aspects of the development—or rather nondevelopment—of the US welfare state. Slave Capital and Human Capital I have not tried to estimate the value of slave capital in other slave societies. In the British Empire, slavery was abolished in 1833–1838. In the French Empire it was abolished in two stages (first abolished in 1792, restored by Napoleon in 1803, abolished definitively in 1848). In both empires, in the eighteenth and early nineteenth centuries a portion of foreign capital was invested in plantations in the West Indies (think of Sir Thomas in Mansfield Park) or in slave estates on islands in the Indian Ocean (the Ile Bourbon and Ile de France, which became Réunion and Mauritius after the French Revolution). Among the assets of these plantations were slaves, whose value I have not attempted to calculate separately. Since total foreign assets did not exceed 10 percent of national income in these two countries at the beginning of the nineteenth century, the share of slaves in total wealth was obviously smaller than in the United States. Conversely, in societies where slaves represent a large share of the population, their market value can easily reach very high levels, potentially even higher than it did in the United States in 1770–1810 and greater than the value of all other forms of wealth. Take an extreme case in which virtually an entire population is owned by a tiny minority. Assume for the sake of argument that the income from labor (that is, the yield to slave owners on the labor of their slaves) represents 60 percent of national income, the income on capital (meaning the return on land and other capital in the form of rents, profits, etc.) represents 40 percent of national income, and the return on all forms of nonhuman capital is 5 percent a year.

By definition, the value of national capital (excluding slaves) is equal to eight years of national income: this is the first fundamental law of capitalism ($\beta = \alpha / r$), introduced in Chapter 1. In a slave society, we can apply the same law to slave capital: if slaves yield the equivalent of 60 percent of national income, and the return on all forms of capital is 5 percent a year, then the market value of the total stock of slaves is equal to twelve years of national income—or half again more than 16 national nonhuman capital, simply because slaves yield half again as much as nonhuman capital. If weadd the value of slaves to the value of capital, we of course obtain twenty years of national income,since the total annual flow of income and output is capitalized at a rate of 5 percent. In the case of the United States in the period 1770–1810, the value of slave capital was on theorder of one and a half years of national income (and not twelve years), in part because theproportion of slaves in the population was 20 percent (and not 100 percent) and in part because theaverage productivity of slaves was slightly below the average productivity of free labor and the rateof return on slave capital was generally closer to 7 or 8 percent, or even higher, than it was to 5percent, leading to a lower capitalization. In practice, in the antebellum United States, the marketprice of a slave was typically on the order of ten to twelve years of an equivalent free worker'swages (and not twenty years, as equal productivity and a return of 5 percent would require). In 1860,the average price of a male slave of prime working age was roughly $2,000, whereas the averagewage of a free farm laborer was on the order of $200. Note, however, that the price of a slavevaried widely depending on various characteristics and on the owner's evaluation; for example, thewealthy planter Quentin Tarantino portrays in Django Unchained is prepared to sell beautifulBroomhilda for only $700 but wants $12,000 for his best fighting slaves. In any case, it is clear that this type of calculation makes sense only in a slave society, wherehuman capital can be sold on the market, permanently and irrevocably. Some economists, includingthe authors of a recent series of World Bank reports on "the wealth of nations," choose to calculatethe total value of "human capital" by capitalizing the value of the income flow from labor on the basisof a more or less arbitrary annual rate of return (typically 4–5 percent). These reports conclude withamazement that human capital is the leading form of capital in the enchanted world of the twenty-firstcentury. In reality, this conclusion is perfectly obvious and would also have been true in theeighteenth century: whenever more than half of national income goes to labor and one chooses tocapitalize the flow of labor income at the same or nearly the same rate as the flow of income tocapital, then by definition the value of human capital is greater than the value of all other forms ofcapital. There is no need for amazement and no need to resort to a hypothetical capitalization to reachthis conclusion. (It is enough to compare the flows.). Attributing a monetary value to the stock ofhuman capital makes sense only in societies where it is actually possible to own other individualsfully and entirely—societies that at first sight have definitively ceased to exist.

CHAPTER FIVE

The Capital/Income Ratio over the Long Run

Over the long run, the nature of wealth was totally transformed: capital in the form of agricultural land was gradually replaced by industrial and financial capital and urban real estate. Yet the most striking fact was surely that in spite of these transformations, the total value of the capital stock, measured in years of national income—the ratio that measures the overall importance of capital in the economy and society—appears not to have changed very much over a very long period of time. In Britain and France, the countries for which we possess the most complete historical data, national capital today represents about five or six years of national income, which is just slightly less than the level of wealth observed in the eighteenth and nineteenth centuries and right up to the eve of World War I (about six or seven years of national income). Given the strong, steady increase of the capital/income ratio since the 1950s, moreover, it is natural to ask whether this increase will continue in the decades to come and whether the capital/income ratio will regain or even surpass past levels before the end of the twenty-first century. The second salient fact concerns the comparison between Europe and the United States. Unsurprisingly, the shocks of the 1914–1945 period affected Europe much more strongly, so that the capital/income ratio was lower there from the 1920s into the 1980s. If we except this lengthy period of war and its aftermath, however, we find that the capital/income ratio has always tended to be higher in Europe. This was true in the nineteenth and early twentieth centuries (when the capital/income ratio was 6 to 7 in Europe compared with 4 to 5 in the United States) and again in the late twentieth and early twenty-first centuries: private wealth in Europe again surpassed US levels in the early 1990s, and the capital/income ratio there is close to 6 today, compared with slightly more than 4 in the United States

These facts remain to be explained. Why did the capital/income ratio return to historical highs in Europe, and why should it be structurally higher in Europe than in the United States? What magical forces imply that capital in one society should be worth six or seven years of national income rather than three or four? Is there an equilibrium level for the capital/income ratio, and if so how is it determined, what are the consequences for the rate of return on capital, and what is the relation between it and the capital-labor split of national income? To answer these questions, I will begin by presenting the dynamic law that allows us to relate the capital/income ratio in an economy to its savings and growth rates. The Second Fundamental Law of Capitalism: $\beta = s / g$ In the long run, the capital/income ratio β is related in a simple and transparent way to the savings rate s and the growth rate g according to the following formula: $\beta = s / g$ For example, if $s = 12\%$ and $g = 2\%$, then $\beta = s / g = 600\%$. In other words, if a country saves 12 percent of its national income every year, and the rate of growth of its national income is 2 percent per year, then in the long run the capital/income ratio will be equal to 600 percent: the country will have accumulated capital worth six years of national income. This formula, which can be regarded as the second fundamental law of capitalism, reflects an obvious but important point: a country that saves a lot and grows slowly will over the long run accumulate an enormous stock of capital (relative to its income), which can in turn have a significant effect on the social structure and distribution of wealth. Let me put it another way: in a quasi-stagnant society, wealth accumulated in the past will inevitably acquire disproportionate importance. The return to a structurally high capital/income ratio in the twenty-first century, close to the levels observed in the eighteenth and nineteenth centuries, can therefore be explained by the return to a 2 slow-growth regime. Decreased growth—especially demographic growth—is thus responsible for capital's comeback. The basic point is that small variations in the rate of growth can have very large effects on the capital/income ratio over the long run. For example, given a savings rate of 12 percent, if the rate of growth falls to 1.5 percent a year (instead of 2 percent), then the long-term capital/income ratio $\beta = s / g$ will rise to eight years of national income (instead of six). If the growth rate falls to 1 percent, then $\beta = s / g$ will rise to twelve years, indicative of a society twice as capital intensive as when the growth rate was 2 percent. In one respect, this is good news: capital is potentially useful to everyone, and provided that things are properly organized, everyone can benefit from it. In another respect, however, what this means is that the owners of capital—for a given distribution of wealth—potentially control a larger share of total economic resources. In any event, the economic, social, and political repercussions of such a change are considerable. On the other hand if the growth rate increases to 3 percent, then $\beta = s / g$ will fall to just four years of national income. If the savings rate simultaneously decreases slightly to $s = 9$ percent, then the long-run capital/income ratio will decline to 3. These effects are all the more significant because the growth rate that figures in the law $\beta = s / g$ is the overall rate of growth of national income, that is, the sum of the per capita growth rate and the population growth rate. In other words, for a savings rate on the order of 10–12 percent and a growth rate of national income per capita on the order of 1.5–2 percent a year, it follows immediately that a country that has near-zero demographic growth and therefore a total growth rate close to 1.5–2 percent, as in Europe, can expect to accumulate a capital stock worth six to eight years of national income, whereas a country with demographic growth on the order of 1 percent a year and therefore a total growth rate of 2.5–3 percent, as in the United States, will accumulate a capital stock worth only three to four years of national income. And if the latter country tends to save a little less than the former, perhaps because its population is not aging as rapidly, this mechanism will be further reinforced as a result. In other words, countries with similar growth rates of income per capita can end up with very different capital/income ratios simply because their demographic growth rates are not the same. This law allows us to give a good account of the historical evolution of the capital/income ratio. In particular, it enables us to explain why the capital/income ratio seems now—after the shocks of 1914–1945 and the exceptionally rapid growth phase of the second half of the twentieth century—to be returning to very high levels. It also enables us to understand why Europe tends for structural reasons to accumulate more capital than the United States (or at any rate will tend to do so as long as the US demographic growth rate remains higher than the European, which probably will not be forever). But before I can explain this phenomenon, I must make several conceptual and theoretical points more precise. A Long-Term Law First, it is important to be clear that the second fundamental law of capitalism, $\beta = s / g$, is applicable only if certain crucial assumptions are satisfied. First, this is an asymptotic law, meaning that it is 3 valid only in the long run: if a country saves a proportion s of its income indefinitely, and if the rate of growth of its national income is g permanently, then its capital/income ratio will tend closer and closer to $\beta = s / g$ and stabilize at that level. This won't happen in a day, however: if a country saves a proportion s of its income for only a few years, it will not be enough to achieve a capital/income ratio of $\beta = s / g$. For example, if a country starts with zero capital and saves 12 percent of its national income for a year, it obviously will not accumulate a capital stock worth six years of its income. With a savings rate of 12 percent a year, starting from zero capital, it will take fifty years to save the equivalent of six years of income, and even then the capital/income ratio will not be equal to 6, because national income will itself have increased considerably after half a century (unless we assume that the growth rate is actually zero). The first principle to bear in mind is, therefore, that the accumulation of wealth takes time: it will take several decades for the law $\beta = s / g$ to become true. Now we can understand why it took so much time for the shocks of 1914–1945 to fade away, and why it is so important to take a very long historical view when studying these questions. At the individual level, fortunes are sometimes amassed very quickly, but at the country level, the movement of the capital/income ratio described by the law $\beta = s / g$ is a long-run phenomenon. Hence there is a crucial difference between this law and the law $\alpha = r \times \beta$, which I called the first fundamental law of capitalism in Chapter 1. According to that law, the share of capital income in national income, α, is equal to the average rate of return on capital, r, times the capital/income ratio, β. It is important to realize that the law $\alpha = r \times \beta$ is actually a pure accounting identity, valid at all times in all places, by construction. Indeed, one can view it as a definition of the share of capital in national income (or of the rate of return on capital, depending on which parameter is easiest to measure) rather than as a law. By contrast, the law $\beta = s / g$ is the result of a dynamic process: it represents a state of equilibrium toward which an economy will tend if the savings rate is s and the growth rate g, but that equilibrium state is never perfectly realized in practice. Second, the law $\beta = s / g$ is valid only if one focuses on those forms of capital that human beings can accumulate. If a significant fraction of national capital consists of pure natural resources (i.e., natural resources whose value is independent of any human improvement and any past investment), then β can be quite high without any contribution from savings. I will say more later about the practical importance of nonaccumulable capital. Finally, the law $\beta = s / g$ is valid only if asset prices evolve on average in the same way as consumer prices. If the price of real estate or stocks rises faster than other prices, then the ratio β between the market value of national capital and the annual flow of national income can again be quite high without the addition of any new savings. In the short run, variations (capital gains or losses) of relative asset prices (i.e., of asset prices relative to consumer prices) are often quite a bit larger than volume effects (i.e., effects linked to new savings). If we assume, however, that price variations balance out over the long run, then the law $\beta = s / g$ is necessarily valid, regardless of the reasons why the country in question chooses to save a proportion s of its national income. This point bears emphasizing: the law $\beta = s / g$ is totally independent of the reasons why the residents of a particular country—or their government—accumulate wealth. In practice, people accumulate capital for all sorts of reasons: for instance, to increase future consumption (or to avoid a decrease in consumption after retirement), or to amass or preserve wealth for the next generation, or again to acquire the power, security, or prestige that often come with wealth. In general, all these motivations are present at once in proportions that vary with the individual, the country, and the age. Quite often, all these motivations are combined in single individuals, and individuals themselves may not always be able to articulate them clearly. In Part Three I discuss in depth the significant implications of these various motivations and mechanisms of accumulation for inequality and the distribution of wealth, the role of inheritance in the structure of inequality, and, more generally, the social, moral, and political justification of disparities in wealth. At this stage I am simply explaining the dynamics of the capital/income ratio (a question that can be studied, at least initially, independently of the question of how wealth is distributed). The point I want to stress is that the law $\beta = s / g$ applies in all cases, regardless of the exact reasons for a country's savings rate. This is due to the simple fact that $\beta = s / g$ is the only stable capital/income ratio in a country that saves a fraction s of its income, which grows at a rate g. The argument is elementary. Let me illustrate it with an example. In concrete terms: if a country is saving 12 percent of its income every year, and if its initial capital stock is equal to six years of income, then the capital stock will grow at 2 percent a year, thus at exactly the same rate as national income, so that the capital/income ratio will remain stable. By contrast, if the capital stock is less than six years of income, then a savings rate of 12 percent will cause the capital stock to grow at a rate greater than 2 percent a year and therefore faster than income, so that the capital/income ratio will increase until it attains its equilibrium level. Conversely, if the capital stock is greater than six years of annual income, then a savings rate of 12 percent implies that capital is growing at less than 2 percent a year, so that the capital/income ratio cannot be maintained at that level and will therefore decrease until it reaches equilibrium. In each case, the capital/income ratio tends over the long run toward its equilibrium level $\beta = s \, / \, g$ (possibly augmented by pure natural resources), provided that the average price of assets evolves at the same rate as consumption prices over the long run. To sum up: the law $\beta = s \, / \, g$ does not explain the short-term shocks to which the capital/income ratio is subject, any more than it explains the existence of world wars or the crisis of 1929—events that can be taken as examples of extreme shocks—but it does allow us to understand the potential equilibrium level toward which the capital/income ratio tends in the long run, when the effects of shocks and crises have dissipated.

In order to illustrate the difference between short-term and long-term movements of the capital/income ratio, it is useful to examine the annual changes observed in the wealthiest countries between 1970 and 2010, a period for which we have reliable and homogeneous data for a large number of countries. To begin, here is a look at the ratio of private capital to national income, whose evolution

richest countries in the world, in order of decreasing GDP: the United States, Japan, Germany, France, Britain, Italy, Canada, and Australia.

These erratic changes are due to the fact that the prices of real estate (including housing and business real estate) and financial assets (especially shares of stock) are notoriously volatile. It is always very difficult to set a price on capital, in part because it is objectively complex to foresee the future demand for the goods and services generated by a firm or by real estate and therefore to predict the future flows of profit, dividends, royalties, rents, and so on that the assets in question will yield, and in part because the present value of a building or corporation depends not only on these fundamental factors but also on the price at which one can hope to sell these assets if the need arises (that is, on the anticipated capital gain or loss). Indeed, these anticipated future prices themselves depend on the general enthusiasm for a given type of asset, which can give rise to so-called self-fulfilling beliefs: as long as one can hope to sell an asset for more than one paid for it, it may be individually rational to pay a good deal more than the fundamental value of that asset (especially since the fundamental value is itself uncertain), thus giving in to the general enthusiasm for that type of asset, even though it may be excessive. That is why speculative bubbles in real estate and stocks have existed as long as capital itself; they are consubstantial with its history. As it happens, the most spectacular bubble in the period 1970–2010 was surely the Japanese bubble of 1990 During the 1980s, the value of private wealth shot up in Japan fromslightly more than four years of national income at the beginning of the decade to nearly seven at the end. Clearly, this enormous and extremely rapid increase was partly artificial: the value of private capital fell sharply in the early 1990s before stabilizing at around six years of national income fromthe mid-1990s on. I will not rehearse the history of the numerous real estate and stock market bubbles that inflated and burst in the rich countries after 1970, nor will I attempt to predict future bubbles, which I am quite incapable of doing in any case. Note, however, the sharp correction in the Italian real estate market in 1994–1995 and the bursting of the Internet bubble in 2000–2001, which caused a particularly sharp drop in the capital/income ratio in the United States and Britain (though not as sharp as the drop in Japan ten years earlier). Note, too, that the subsequent US real estate and stock market boomcontinued until 2007, followed by a deep drop in the recession of 2008–2009. In two years, US private fortunes shrank from five to four years of national income, a drop of roughly the same size as the Japanese correction of 1991–1992. In other countries, and particularly in Europe, the correction was less severe or even nonexistent: in Britain, France, and Italy, the price of assets, especially in real estate, briefly stabilized in 2008 before starting upward again in 2009–2010, so that by the early 2010s private wealth had returned to the level attained in 2007, if not slightly higher. The important point I want to emphasize is that beyond these erratic and unpredictable variations in short-term asset prices, variations whose amplitude seems to have increased in recent decades (and we will see later that this can be related to the increase in the potential capital/income ratio), there is indeed a long-term trend at work in all of the rich countries in the period 1970–2010 (see Figure 5.3). At the beginning of the 1970s, the total value of private wealth (net of debt) stood between two and three and a half years of national income in all the rich countries, on all continents. Forty years later, in 2010, private wealth represented between four and seven years of national income in all the countries under study.

The general evolution is clear: bubbles aside, what we are witnessing is a strong comeback of private capital in the rich countries since 1970, or, to put it another way, the emergence of a new patrimonial capitalism. This structural evolution is explained by three sets of factors, which complement and reinforce one another to give the phenomenon a very significant amplitude. The most important factor in the long run is slower growth, especially demographic growth, which, together with a high rate of saving, automatically gives rise to a structural increase in the long-run capital/income ratio, owing to the law $\beta = s / g$. This mechanism is the dominant force in the very long run but should not be allowed to obscure the two other factors that have substantially reinforced its effects over the last few decades: first, the gradual privatization and transfer of public wealth into private hands in the 1970s and 1980s, and second, a long-term catch-up phenomenon affecting real estate and stock market prices, which also accelerated in the 1980s and 1990s in a political context that was on the whole more favorable to private wealth than that of the immediate postwar decades. Beyond Bubbles: Low Growth, High Saving I begin with the first mechanism, based on slower growth coupled with continued high saving and the dynamic law $\beta = s / g$.

I have indicated the average values of the growth rates and private savings rates in the eight richest countries during the period 1970–2010.

For the sake of completeness, I should make clear that private saving consists of two components: savings made directly by private individuals (this is the part of disposable household income that is not consumed immediately) and savings by firms on behalf of the private individuals who own them, directly in the case of individual firms or indirectly via their financial investments. This second component consists of profits reinvested by firms (also referred to as "retained earnings") and in some countries accounts for as much as half the total amount of private savings If one were to ignore this second component of savings and consider only household savings strictly defined, one would conclude that savings flows in all countries are clearly insufficient to account for the growth of private wealth, which one would then explain largely in terms of a structural increase in the relative price of assets, especially shares of stock. Such a conclusion would be correct in accounting terms but artificial in economic terms: it is true that stock prices tend to rise more quickly than consumption prices over the long run, but the reason for this is essentially that retained earnings allow firms to increase their size and capital (so that we are looking at a volume effect rather than a price effect). If retained earnings are included in private savings, however, the price effect largely disappears.

In practice, from the standpoint of shareholders, profits paid out directly as dividends are often more heavily taxed than retained earnings: hence it may be advantageous for the owners of capital to pay only a limited share of profits as dividends (to meet their immediate consumption needs) and leave the rest to accumulate and be reinvested in the firm and its subsidiaries. Later, some shares can be sold in order to realize the capital gains (which are generally taxed less heavily than dividends). The variation between countries with respect to the proportion of retained earnings in total private savings can be explained, moreover, largely by differences in legal and tax systems; these are accounting differences rather than actual economic differences. Under these conditions, it is better to treat retained earnings as savings realized on behalf of the firm's owners and therefore as a component of private saving. I should also be clear that the notion of savings relevant to the dynamic law $\beta = s\,/\,g$ is savings net of capital depreciation, that is, truly new savings, or the part of total savings left over after we deduct the amount needed to compensate for wear and tear on buildings and equipment (to repair a hole in the roof or a pipe or to replace a worn-out automobile, computer, machine, or what have you). The difference is important, because annual capital depreciation in the developed economies is on the order of 10–15 percent of national income and absorbs nearly half of total savings, which generally run around 25–30 percent of national income, leaving net savings of 10–15 percent of national income

In particular, the bulk of retained earnings often goes to maintaining buildings and equipment, and frequently the amount left over to finance net investment is quite small—at most a few percent of national income—or even negative, if retained earnings are insufficient to cover the depreciation of capital. By definition, only net savings can increase the capital stock: savings used to cover depreciation simply ensure that the existing capital stock will not decrease.

Finally, I want to make it clear that private saving as defined here, and therefore private wealth, does not include household purchases of durable goods: furniture, appliances, automobiles, and so on. In this respect I am following international standards for national accounting, under which durable household goods are treated as items of immediate consumption (although the same goods, when purchased by firms, are counted as investments with a high rate of annual depreciation). This is of limited importance for my purposes, however, because durable goods have always represented a relatively small proportion of total wealth, which has not varied much over time: in all rich countries, available estimates indicate that the total value of durable household goods is generally between 30 and 50 percent of national income throughout the period 1970–2010, with no apparent trend. In other words, everyone owns on average between a third and half a year's income worth of furniture, refrigerators, cars, and so on, or 10,000–15,000 euros per capita for a national income on the order of 30,000 euros per capita in the early 2010s. This is not a negligible amount and accounts for most of the wealth owned by a large segment of the population. Compared, however, with overall private wealth of five to six years of national income, or 150,000–200,000 euros per person (excluding durable goods), about half of which is in the form of real estate and half in net financial assets (bank deposits, stocks, bonds, and other investments, net of debt) and business capital, this is only a small supplementary amount. Concretely, if we were to include durable goods in private wealth, the only effect would be to add 30–50 percent of national income to the curves shown in Figure 5.3 without significantly modifying the overall evolution. Note in passing that apart from real estate and business capital, the only nonfinancial assets included in national accounts under international standards (which I have followed scrupulously in order to ensure consistency in my comparisons of private and national wealth between countries) are "valuables," including items such as works of art, jewelry, and precious metals such as gold and silver, which households acquire as a pure reservoir of value (or for their aesthetic value) and which in principle do not deteriorate (or deteriorate very little) over time. These valuables are worth much 13 less than durable goods by most estimates, however (between 5 and 10 percent of national income, depending on the country, or between 1,500 and 3,000 per person for a per capita national income of 30,000 euros), hence their share of total private wealth is relatively small, even after the recent rise in the price of gold. It is interesting to note that according to available historical estimates, these orders of magnitude do not seem to have changed much over the long run. Estimates of the value of durable goods are generally around 30–50 percent of national income for both the nineteenth and twentieth centuries. Gregory King's estimates of British national wealth around 1700 show the same thing: the total value of furniture, china, and so on was about 30 percent of national income. The amount of wealth represented by valuables and precious objects seems to have decreased over the long run, however, from 10–15 percent of national income in the late nineteenth and early twentieth century to 5–10 percent today. According to King, the total value of such goods (including metal coin) was as high as 25–30 percent of national income around 1700. In all cases, these are relatively limited amounts compared to total accumulated wealth in Britain of around seven years of national income, primarily in the form of farmland, dwellings, and other capital goods (shops, factories, warehouses, livestock, ships, etc.), at which King does not fail to rejoice and marvel. Private Capital Expressed in Years of Disposable Income Note, moreover, that the capital/income ratio would have attained even higher levels—no doubt the highest ever recorded—in the rich countries in the 2000s and 2010s if I had expressed total private wealth in terms of years of disposable income rather than national income, as I have done thus far. This seemingly technical issue warrants further discussion. As the name implies, disposable household income (or simply "disposable income") measures the monetary income that households in a given country dispose of directly. To go from national income to disposable income, one must deduct all taxes, fees, and other obligatory payments and add all monetary transfers (pensions, unemployment insurance, aid to families, welfare payments, etc.). Until the turn of the twentieth century, governments played a limited role in social and economic life (total tax payments were on the order of 10 percent of national income, which went essentially to pay for traditional state functions such as police, army, courts, highways, and so on, so that disposable income was generally around 90 percent of national income). The state's role increased considerably over the course of the twentieth century, so that disposable income today amounts to around 70–80 percent of national income in the rich countries. As a result, total private wealth expressed in years of disposable income (rather than national income) is significantly higher. For example, private capital in the 2000s represented four to seven years of national income in the rich countries, which would correspond to five to nine years of disposable income.

Both ways of measuring the capital/income ratio can be justified, depending on how one wants to approach the question. When expressed in terms of disposable income, the ratio emphasizes strictly monetary realities and shows us the magnitude of wealth in relation to the income actually available to households (to save, for instance). In a way, this reflects the concrete reality of the family bank account, and it is important to keep these orders of magnitude in mind. It is also important to note, however, that the gap between disposable income and national income measures by definition the value of public services from which households benefit, especially health and education services financed directly by the public treasury. Such "transfers in kind" are just as valuable as the monetary transfers included in disposable income: they allow the individuals concerned to avoid spending comparable (or even greater) sums on private producers of health and education services. Ignoring such transfers in kind might well distort certain evolutions or international comparisons. That is why it seemed to me preferable to express wealth in years of national income: to do so is to adopt an economic (rather than strictly monetary) view of income. In this book, whenever I refer to the capital/income ratio without further qualification, I am always referring to the ratio of the capital stock to the flow of national income. The Question of Foundations and Other Holders of Capital Note also that for the sake of completeness I have included in private wealth not only the assets and liabilities of private individuals ("households" in national accounting terminology) but also assets and liabilities held by foundations and other nonprofit organizations. To be clear, this category includes only foundations and other organizations financed primarily by gifts from private individuals or income from their properties. Organizations that depend primarily on public subsidies are classified as governmental organizations, and those that depend primarily on the sale of goods are classified as corporations. In practice, all of these distinctions are malleable and porous. It is rather arbitrary to count the wealth of foundations as part of private wealth rather than public wealth or to place it in a category of its own, since it is in fact a novel form of ownership, intermediate between purely private and strictly 16 public ownership. In practice, when we think of the property owned by churches over the centuries, or the property owned today by organizations such as Doctors without Borders or the Bill and Melinda Gates Foundation, it is clear that we are dealing with a wide variety of moral persons pursuing a range of specific objectives. Note, however, that the stakes are relatively limited, since the amount of wealth owned by moral persons is generally rather small compared with what physical persons retain for themselves. Available estimates for the various rich countries in the period 1970–2010 show that foundations and other nonprofit organizations always own less than 10 percent and generally less than 5 percent of total private wealth, though with interesting variations between countries: barely 1 percent in

France, around 3–4 percent in Japan, and as much as 6–7 percent in the United States (with no apparent trend). Available historical sources indicate that the total value of church-owned property in eighteenth-century France amounted to about 7–8 percent of total private wealth, or approximately 50–60 percent of national income (some of this property was confiscated and sold during the French Revolution to pay off debts incurred by the government of the Ancien Régime). In other words, the Catholic Church owned more property in Ancien Régime France (relative to the total private wealth of the era) than prosperous US foundations own today. It is interesting to observe that the two levels are nevertheless fairly close. These are quite substantial holdings of wealth, especially if we compare them with the meager (and sometimes negative) net wealth owned by the government at various points in time. Compared with total private wealth, however, the wealth of foundations remains fairly modest. In particular, it matters little whether or not we include foundations when considering the general evolution of the ratio of private capital to national income over the long run. Inclusion is justified, moreover, by the fact that it is never easy to define the boundary line between on the one hand various legal structures such as foundations, trust funds, and the like used by wealthy individuals to manage their assets and further their private interests (which are in principle counted in national accounts as individual holdings, assuming they are identified as such) and on the other hand foundations and nonprofits said to be in the public interest. I will come back to this delicate issue in Part Three, where I will discuss the dynamics of global inequality of wealth, and especially great wealth, in the twenty-first century. The Privatization of Wealth in the Rich Countries The very sharp increase in private wealth observed in the rich countries, and especially in Europe and Japan, between 1970 and 2010 thus can be explained largely by slower growth coupled with continued high savings, using the law $\beta = s \, / \, g$. I will now return to the two other complementary phenomena that amplified this mechanism, which I mentioned earlier: the privatization or gradual transfer of public wealth into private hands and the "catch-up" of asset prices over the long run.

I begin with privatization. As noted, the proportion of public capital in national capital has dropped sharply in recent decades, especially in France and Germany, where net public wealth represented as much as a quarter or even a third of total national wealth in the period 1950–1970, whereas today it represents just a few percent (public assets are just enough to balance public debt). This evolution reflects a quite general phenomenon that has affected all eight leading developed economies: a gradual decrease in the ratio of public capital to national income in the period 1970–2010, accompanied by an increase in the ratio of private capital to national income (see Figure 5.5). In other words, the revival of private wealth is partly due to the privatization of national wealth. To be sure, the increase in private capital in all countries was greater than the decrease in public capital, so national capital (measured in years of national income) did indeed increase. But it increased less rapidly than private capital owing to privatization. The case of Italy is particularly clear. Net public wealth was slightly positive in the 1970s, then turned slightly negative in the 1980s as large government deficits mounted. All told, public wealth decreased by an amount equal to nearly a year of national income over the period 1970–2010. At the same time, private wealth rose from barely two and a half years of national income in 1970 to nearly seven in 2010, an increase of roughly four and a half years. In other words, the decrease in public wealth represented between one-fifth and one-quarter of the increase in private wealth—a nonnegligible share. Italian national wealth did indeed rise significantly, from around two and a half years of national income in 1970 to about six in 2010, but this was a smaller increase than in private wealth, whose exceptional growth was to some extent misleading, since nearly a quarter of it reflected a growing debt that one portion of the Italian population owed to another. Instead of paying taxes to balance the government's budget, the Italians—or at any rate those who had the means—lent money to the government by buying government bonds or public assets, which increased their private wealth without increasing the national wealth. Indeed, despite a very high rate of private saving (roughly 15 percent of national income), national saving in Italy was less than 10 percent of national income in the period 1970–2010. In other words, more than a third of private saving was absorbed by government deficits. A similar pattern exists in all the rich countries, but one generally less extreme than in Italy: in most countries, public saving was negative (which means that public investment was less than the public deficit: the government invested less than it borrowed or used borrowed money to pay current expenses). In France, Britain, Germany, and the United States, government deficits exceeded public investment by 2–3 percent of national income on average over the period 1970–2010, compared with more than 6 percent in Italy (see Table 5.4). In all the rich countries, public dissaving and the consequent decrease in public wealth accounted for a significant portion of the increase in private wealth (between one-tenth and one-quarter, depending on the country). This was not the primary reason for the increase in private wealth, but it should not be neglected. It is possible, moreover, that the available estimates somewhat undervalue public assets in the 1970s, especially in Britain (and perhaps Italy and France as well), which would lead us to underestimate the magnitude of the transfers of public wealth to private hands. If true, this would allow us to explain why British private wealth increased so much between 1970 and 2010, despite a clearly insufficient private savings rate, and in particular during the waves of privatizations of public firms in the 1980s and 1990s, privatizations that often involved notoriously low prices, which of course guaranteed that the policy would be popular with buyers.

It is important to note that these transfers of public sector wealth to the private sector were not limited to rich countries after 1970—far from it. The same general pattern exists on all continents. At the global level, the most extensive privatization in recent decades, and indeed in the entire history of capital, obviously took place in the countries of the former Soviet bloc. The highly imperfect estimates available to us indicate that private wealth in Russia and the former Eastern bloc countries stood at about four years of national income in the late 2000s and early 2010s, and net public wealth was extremely low, just as in the rich countries. Available estimates for the 1970s and 1980s, prior to the fall of the Berlin Wall and the collapse of the Communist regimes, are 18 19 even more imperfect, but all signs are that the distribution was strictly the opposite: private wealth was insignificant (limited to individual plots of land and perhaps some housing in the Communist countries least averse to private property but in all cases less than a year's national income), and public capital represented the totality of industrial capital and the lion's share of national capital, amounting, as a first approximation, to between three and four years of national income. In other words, at first sight, the stock of national capital did not change, but the public-private split was totally reversed. To sum up: the very considerable growth of private wealth in Russia and Eastern Europe between the late 1980s and the present, which led in some cases to the spectacularly rapid enrichment of certain individuals (I am thinking mainly of the Russian "oligarchs"), obviously had nothing to do with saving or the dynamic law $\beta = s\,/\,g$. It was purely and simply the result of a transfer of ownership of capital from the government to private individuals. The privatization of national wealth in the developed countries since 1970 can be regarded as a very attenuated form of this extreme case. The Historic

Rebound of Asset Prices The last factor explaining the increase in the capital/income ratio over the past few decades is the historic rebound of asset prices. In other words, no correct analysis of the period 1970–2010 is possible unless we situate this period in the longer historical context of 1910–2010. Complete historical records are not available for all developed countries, but the series I have established for Britain, France, Germany, and the United States yield consistent results, which I summarize below. If we look at the whole period 1910–2010, or 1870–2010, we find that the global evolution of the capital/income ratio is very well explained by the dynamic law $\beta = s\,/\,g$. In particular, the fact that the capital/income ratio is structurally higher over the long run in Europe than in the United States is perfectly consistent with the differences in the saving rate and especially the growth rate over the past century. The decline we see in the period 1910–1950 is consistent with low national savings and wartime destruction, and the fact that the capital/income ratio rose more rapidly between 1980 and 2010 than between 1950 and 1980 is well explained by the decrease in the growth rate between these two periods. Nevertheless, the low point of the 1950s was lower than the simple logic of accumulation summed up by the law $\beta = s\,/\,g$ would have predicted. In order to understand the depth of the mid-twentiethcentury low, we need to add the fact that the price of real estate and stocks fell to historically low levels in the aftermath of World War II for any number of reasons (rent control laws, financial regulation, a political climate unfavorable to private capitalism). After 1950, these asset prices gradually recovered, with an acceleration after 1980. According to my estimates, this historical catch-up process is now complete: leaving aside erratic short-term price movements, the increase in asset prices between 1950 and 2010 seems broadly speaking to have compensated for the decline between 1910 and 1950. It would be risky to conclude from this that the phase of structural asset price increases is definitively over, however, and that asset prices will henceforth progress at exactly the same pace as consumer prices. For one thing, the historical sources are incomplete and imperfect, and price comparisons over such long periods of time are approximate at best. For another, there are many theoretical reasons why asset prices may 20 evolve differently from other prices over the long run: for example, some types of assets, such as buildings and infrastructure, are affected by technological progress at a rate different from those of other parts of the economy. Furthermore, the fact that certain natural resources are nonrenewable can also be important. Last but not least, it is important to stress that the price of capital, leaving aside the perennial shortand medium-term bubbles and possible long-term structural divergences, is always in part a social and political construct: it reflects each society's notion of property and depends on the many policies and institutions that regulate relations among different social groups, and especially between those who own capital and those who do not. This is obvious, for example, in the case of real estate prices, which depend on laws regulating the relations between landlords and tenants and controlling rents. The law also affects stock market prices, as I noted when I discussed why stock prices in Germany are relatively low. In this connection, it is interesting to analyze the ratio between the stock market value and the accounting value of firms in the period 1970–2010 in those countries for which such data are available.

The market value of a company listed on the stock exchange is its stock market capitalization. For companies not so listed, either because they are too small or because they choose not to finance themselves via the stock market (perhaps in order to preserve family ownership, which can happen even in very large firms), the market value is calculated for national accounting purposes with reference to observed stock prices for listed firms as similar as possible (in terms of size, sector of activity, and so on) to the unlisted firm, while taking into account the "liquidity" of the relevant market. Thus far I have used market values to measure stocks of private wealth and national wealth. The accounting value of a firm, also called book value or net assets or own capital, is equal to the accumulated value of all assets—buildings, infrastructure, machinery, patents, majority or minority stakes in subsidiaries and other firms, vault cash, and so on—included in the firm's balance sheet, less the total of all outstanding debt.

In theory, in the absence of all uncertainty, the market value and book value of a firm should be the 21 same, and the ratio of the two should therefore be equal to 1 (or 100 percent). This is normally the case when a company is created. If the shareholders subscribe to 100 million euros worth of shares, which the firm uses to buy offices and equipment worth 100 million euros, then the market value and book value will both be equal to 100 million euros. The same is true if the firm borrows 50 million euros to buy new machinery worth 50 million euros: the net asset value will still be 100 million euros (150 million in assets minus 50 million in debt), as will the stock market capitalization. The same will be true if the firm earns 50 million in profits and decides to create a reserve to finance new investments worth 50 million: the stock price will rise by the same amount (because everyone knows that the firm has new assets), so that both the market value and the book value will increase to 150 million. The difficulty arises from the fact that anticipating the future of the firm quickly becomes more complex and uncertain. After a certain time, for example, no one is really sure whether the investment of 50 million euros several years earlier is really economically useful to the firm. The book value may then diverge from the market value. The firm will continue to list investments—in new offices, machinery, infrastructure, patents, and so on—on its balance sheet at their market value, so the book value of the firm remains unchanged. The market value of the firm, that is, its stock market capitalization, may be significantly lower or higher, depending on whether financial markets have suddenly become more optimistic or pessimistic about the firm's ability to use its investments to generate new business and profits. That is why, in practice, one always observes enormous variations in the ratio of the market value to the book value of individual firms. This ratio, which is also known as "Tobin's Q" (for the economist James Tobin, who was the first to define it), varied from barely 20 percent to more than 340 percent for French firms listed in the CAC 40 in 2012. It is more difficult to understand why Tobin's Q, when measured for all firms in a given country taken together, should be systematically greater or smaller than 1. Classically, two explanations have been given. If certain immaterial investments (such as expenditures to increase the value of a brand or for research and development) are not counted on the balance sheet, then it is logical for the market value to be structurally greater than the book value. This may explain the ratios slightly greater than 1 observed in the United States (100–120 percent) and especially Britain (120–140 percent) in the late 1990s and 2000s. But these ratios greater than 1 also reflect stock market bubbles in both countries: Tobin's Q fell rapidly toward 1 when the Internet bubble burst in 2001–2002 and in the financial crisis of 2008–2009

Conversely, if the stockholders of a company do not have full control, say, because they have to compromise in a long-term relationship with other "stakeholders" (such as worker representatives, local or national governments, consumer groups, and so on), as we saw earlier is the case in "Rhenish capitalism," then it is logical that the market value should be structurally less than the book value. This may explain the ratios slightly below one observed in France (around 80 percent) and especially Germany and Japan (around 50–70 percent) in the 1990s and 2000s, when English and US firms were at or above 100 percent .Note, too, that stock market capitalization is calculated on the basis of prices observed in current stock transactions, which generally correspond to buyers seeking small minority positions and not buyers seeking to take control of the firm. In the latter case, it 22 23 is common to pay a price significantly higher than the current market price, typically on the order of 20 percent higher. This difference may be enough to explain a Tobin's Q of around 80 percent, even when there are no stakeholders other than minority shareholders. Leaving aside these interesting international variations, which reflect the fact that the price of capital always depends on national rules and institutions, one can note a general tendency for Tobin's Q to increase in the rich countries since 1970. This is a consequence of the historic rebound of asset prices. All told, if we take account of both higher stock prices and higher real estate prices, we can say that the rebound in asset prices accounts for one-quarter to one-third of the increase in the ratio of national capital to national income in the rich countries between 1970 and 2010 (with large variations between countries). National Capital and Net Foreign Assets in the Rich Countries As noted, the enormous amounts of foreign assets held by the rich countries, especially Britain and France, on the eve of World War I totally disappeared following the shocks of 1914–1945, and net foreign asset positions have never returned to their previous high levels. In fact, if we look at the levels of national capital and net foreign capital in the rich countries between 1970 and 2010, it is tempting to conclude that foreign assets were of limited importance. The net foreign asset position is sometimes slightly positive and sometimes slightly negative, depending on the country and the year, but the balance is generally fairly small compared with total national capital. In other words, the sharp increase in the level of national capital in the rich countries reflects mainly the increase of domestic capital, and to a first approximation net foreign assets would seem to have played only a relatively minor role.

This conclusion is not quite accurate, however. For example, Japan and Germany have accumulated quite significant quantities of net foreign assets over the past few decades, especially in the 2000s (largely as an automatic consequence of their trade surpluses). In the early 2010s, Japan's net foreign assets totaled about 70 percent of national income, and Germany's amounted to nearly 50 percent. To be sure, these amounts are still substantially lower than the net foreign assets of Britain and France on 24 the eve of World War I (nearly two years of national income for Britain and more than one for France). Given the rapid pace of accumulation, however, it is natural to ask whether this will continue. To what extent will some countries find themselves owned by other countries over the course of the twenty-first century? Are the substantial net foreign asset positions observed in the colonial era likely to return or even to be surpassed? To deal correctly with this question, we need to bring the petroleum exporting countries and emerging economies (starting with China) back into the analysis. Although historical data concerning these countries is limited (which is why I have not discussed them much to this point), our sources for the current period are much more satisfactory. We must also consider inequality within and not just between countries. I therefore defer this question, which concerns the dynamics of the global distribution of capital, to Part Three. At this stage, I note simply that the logic of the law $\beta = s / g$ can automatically give rise to very large international capital imbalances, as the Japanese case clearly illustrates. For a given level of development, slight differences in growth rates (particularly demographic growth rates) or savings rates can leave some countries with a much higher capital/income ratio than others, in which case it is natural to expect that the former will invest massively in the latter. This can create serious political tensions. The Japanese case also indicates a second type of risk, which can arise when the equilibrium capital/income ratio $\beta = s / g$ rises to a very high level. If the residents of the country in question strongly prefer domestic assets—say, Japanese real estate—this can drive the price of those preferred assets to unprecedentedly high levels. In this respect, it is interesting to note that the Japanese record of 1990 was recently beaten by Spain, where the total amount of net private capital reached eight years of national income on the eve of the crisis of 2007–2008, which is a year more than in Japan in 1990. The Spanish bubble began to shrink quite rapidly in 2010–2011, just as the Japanese bubble did in the early 1990s. It is quite possible that even more spectacular bubbles will form in the future, as the potential capital/income ratio $\beta = s / g$ rises to new heights. In passing, note how useful it is to represent the historical evolution of the capital/income ratio in this way and thus to exploit stocks and flows in the national accounts. Doing so might make it possible to detect obvious overvaluations in time to apply prudential policies and financial regulations designed to temper the speculative enthusiasm of financial institutions in the relevant countries. One should also note that small net positions may hide enormous gross positions. Indeed, one characteristic of today's financial globalization is that every country is to a large extent owned by other countries, which not only distorts perceptions of the global distribution of wealth but also represents an important vulnerability for smaller countries as well as a source of instability in the global distribution of net positions. Broadly speaking, the 1970s and 1980s witnessed an extensive "financialization" of the global economy, which altered the structure of wealth in the sense that the total amount of financial assets and liabilities held by various sectors (households, corporations, government agencies) increased more rapidly than net wealth. In most countries, the total amount of financial assets and liabilities in the early 1970s did not exceed four to five years of national income. By 2010, this amount had increased to ten to fifteen years of national income (in the United States, Japan, Germany, and France in particular) and to twenty years of national income in Britain, which set an absolute historical record. This reflects the unprecedented development of cross-investments 25 26 27 28 involving financial and nonfinancial corporations in the same country (and, in particular, a significant inflation of bank balance sheets, completely out of proportion with the growth of the banks' own capital), as well as cross-investments between countries. In this respect, note that the phenomenon of international cross-investments is much more prevalent in European countries, led by Britain, Germany, and France (where financial assets held by other countries represent between one-quarter and one-half of total domestic financial assets, which is considerable), than in larger economies such as the United States and Japan (where the proportion of foreign-held assets is not much more than one-tenth). This increases the feeling of dispossession, especially in Europe, in part for good reasons, though often to an exaggerated degree. (People quickly forget that while domestic companies and government debt are largely owned by the rest of the world, residents hold equivalent assets abroad through annuities and other financial products.) Indeed, balance sheets structured in this way subject small countries, especially in Europe, to an important vulnerability, in that small "errors" in the valuation of financial assets and liabilities can lead to enormous variations in the net foreign asset position. Furthermore, the evolution of a country's net foreign asset position is determined not only by the accumulation of trade surpluses or deficits but also by very large variations in the return on the country's financial assets and liabilities. I should also point out that these international positions are in substantial part the result of fictitious financial flows associated not with the needs of the real economy but rather with tax optimization strategies and regulatory arbitrage (using screen corporations set up in countries where the tax structure and/or regulatory environment is particularly attractive). I come back to these questions in Part Three, where I will examine the importance of tax havens in the global dynamics of wealth distribution. What Will the Capital/Income Ratio Be in the Twenty-First Century? The dynamic law $\beta = s / g$ also enables us to think about what level the global capital/income ratio might attain in the twenty-first century. First consider what we can say about the past. Concerning Europe (or at any rate the leading economies of Western Europe) and North America, we have reliable estimates for the entire period 1870–2010. For Japan, we have no comprehensive estimate of total private or national wealth prior to 1960, but the incomplete data we do have, in particular Japanese probate records going back to 1905, clearly show that Japanese wealth can be described by the same type of "U-curve" as in Europe, and that the capital/income ratio in the period 1910–1930 rose quite high, to 600–700 percent, before falling to just 200–300 percent in the 1950s and 1960s and then rebounding spectacularly to levels again close to 600–700 percent in the 1990s and 2000s. For other countries and continents, including Asia (apart from Japan), Africa, and South America, relatively complete estimates exist from 1990 on, and these show a capital/income ratio of about four years on average. For the period 1870–1990 there are no truly reliable estimates, and I have simply assumed that the overall level was about the same. Since these countries account for just over a fifth of global output throughout this period, their impact on the global capital/income ratio is in any case fairly limited. The results I have obtained are shown in Figure 5.8. Given the weight of the rich countries in this total, it comes as no surprise to discover that the global capital/income ratio followed the same type 29 30 31 32 of "U-curve": it seems today to be close to 500 percent, which is roughly the same level as that attained on the eve of World War I. The most interesting question concerns the extrapolation of this curve into the future. Here I have used the demographic and economic growth predictions presented in Chapter 2, according to which global output will gradually decline from the current 3 percent a year to just 1.5 percent in the second half of the twenty-first century. I also assume that the savings rate will stabilize at about 10 percent in the long run. With these assumptions, the dynamic law $\beta = s / g$ implies that the global capital/income ratio will quite logically continue to rise and could approach 700 percent before the end of the twenty-first century, or approximately the level observed in

Europe from the eighteenth century to the Belle Époque. In other words, by 2100, the entire planet could look like Europe at the turn of the twentieth century, at least in terms of capital intensity. Obviously, this is just one possibility among others. As noted, these growth predictions are extremely uncertain, as is the prediction of the rate of saving. These simulations are nevertheless plausible and valuable as a way of illustrating the crucial role of slower growth in the accumulation of capital.

The Mystery of Land Values By definition, the law $\beta = s / g$ applies only to those forms of capital that can be accumulated. It does not take account of the value of pure natural resources, including "pure land," that is, land prior to any human improvements. The fact that the law $\beta = s / g$ allows us to explain nearly the entirety of the observed capital stock in 2010 (between 80 and 100 percent, depending on the country) suggests that pure land constitutes only a small part of national capital. But exactly how much? The available data are insufficient to give a precise answer to this question. Consider first the case of farmland in a traditional rural society. It is very difficult to say precisely what portion of its value represents "pure land value" prior to any human exploitation and what corresponds to the many investments in and improvements to this land over the centuries (including clearing, drainage, fencing, and so on). In the eighteenth century, the value of farmland in France and Britain attained the equivalent of four years of national income. According to contemporary 33 estimates, investments and improvements represented at least three-quarters of this value and probably more. The value of pure land represented at most one year of national income, and probably less than half a year. This conclusion follows primarily from the fact that the annual value of the labor required to clear, drain, and otherwise improve the land was considerable, on the order of 3–4 percent of national income. With relatively slow growth, less than 1 percent a year, the cumulative value of such investments was undoubtedly close to the total value of the land (if not greater). It is interesting that Thomas Paine, in his famous "Agrarian Justice" proposal to French legislators in 1795, also concluded that "unimproved land" accounted for roughly one-tenth of national wealth, or a little more than half a year of national income. Nevertheless, estimates of this sort are inevitably highly approximate. When the growth rate is low, small variations in the rate of investment produce enormous differences in the long-run value of the capital/income ratio $\beta = s / g$. The key point to remember is that even in a traditional society, the bulk of national capital already stemmed from accumulation and investment: nothing has really changed, except perhaps the fact that the depreciation of land was quite small compared with that of modern real estate or business capital, which has to be repaired or replaced much more frequently. This may contribute to the impression that modern capital is more "dynamic." But since the data we have concerning investment in traditional rural societies are limited and imprecise, it is difficult to say more. In particular, it seems impossible to compare in any precise way the value of pure land long ago with its value today. The principal issue today is urban land: farmland is worth less than 10 percent of national income in both France and Britain. But it is no easier to measure the value of pure urban land today, independent not only of buildings and construction but also of infrastructure and other improvements needed to make the land attractive, than to measure the value of pure farmland in the eighteenth century. According to my estimates, the annual flow of investment over the past few decades can account for almost all the value of wealth, including wealth in real estate, in 2010. In other words, the rise in the capital/income ratio cannot be explained in terms of an increase in the value of pure urban land, which to a first approximation seems fairly comparable to the value of pure farmland in the eighteenth century: half to one year of national income. The margin of uncertainty is nevertheless substantial. Two further points are worth mentioning. First, the fact that total capital, especially in real estate, in the rich countries can be explained fairly well in terms of the accumulation of flows of saving and investment obviously does not preclude the existence of large local capital gains linked to the concentration of population in particular areas, such as major capitals. It would not make much sense to explain the increase in the value of buildings on the Champs-Elysées or, for that matter, anywhere in Paris exclusively in terms of investment flows. Our estimates suggest, however, that these large capital gains on real estate in certain areas were largely compensated by capital losses in other areas, which became less attractive, such as smaller cities or decaying neighborhoods. Second, the fact that the increase in the value of pure land does not seem to explain much of the historic rebound of the capital/income ration in the rich countries in no way implies that this will continue to be true in the future. From a theoretical point of view, there is nothing that guarantees long-term stability of the value of land, much less of all natural resources. I will come back to this 34 point when I analyze the dynamics of wealth and foreign asset holdings in the petroleum exportingcountries.

CHAPTER SIX

From the Capital/Income Ratio to the Capital-Labor Split

I turn now from the analysis of the capital/income ratio to the division of national income between labor and capital. The formula $\alpha = r \times \beta$, which in Chapter 1 I called the first fundamental law of capitalism, allows us to move transparently between the two. For example, if the capital stock is equal to six years of national income ($\beta = 6$), and if the average return on capital is 5 percent a year ($r = 5\%$), then the share of income from capital, α, in national income is 30 percent (and the share of income from labor is therefore 70 percent). Hence the central question is the following: How is the rate of return on capital determined? I shall begin by briefly examining the evolutions observed over the very long run before analyzing the theoretical mechanisms and economic and social forces that come into play. The two countries for which we have the most complete historical data from the eighteenth century on are once again Britain and France.

We find that the general evolution of capital's share of income, α, is described by the same Ushaped curve as the capital/income ratio, β, although the depth of the U is less pronounced. In other words, the rate of return on capital, r, seems to have attenuated the evolution of the quantity of capital, β: r is higher in periods when β is lower, and vice versa, which seems natural. More precisely: we find that capital's share of income was on the order of 35–40 percent in both Britain and France in the late eighteenth century and throughout the nineteenth, before falling to 20–25 percent in the middle of the twentieth century and then rising again to 25–30 percent in the late twentieth and early twenty-first centuries

This corresponds to an average rate of return on capital of around 5–6 percent in the eighteenth and nineteenth centuries, rising to 7–8 percent in the mid-twentieth century, and then falling to 4–5 percent in the late twentieth and early twenty-first centuries

The overall curve and the orders of magnitude described here may be taken as reliable and significant, at least to a first approximation. Nevertheless, the limitations and weaknesses of the data should be noted immediately. First, as noted, the very notion of an "average" rate of return on capital is a fairly abstract construct. In practice, the rate of return varies widely with the type of asset, as well as with the size of individual fortunes (it is generally easier to obtain a good return if one begins with a large stock of capital), and this tends to amplify inequalities. Concretely, the yield on the riskiest assets, including industrial capital (whether in the form of partnerships in family firms in the nineteenth century or shares of stock in listed corporations in the twentieth century), is often greater than 7–8 percent, whereas the yield on less risky assets is significantly lower, on the order of 4–5 percent for farmland in the eighteenth and nineteenth centuries and as low as 3–4 percent for real estate in the early twenty-first century. Small nest eggs held in checking or savings accounts often yield a real rate of return closer to 1–2 percent or even less, perhaps even negative, when the inflation rate exceeds the meager nominal interest rate on such accounts. This is a crucial issue about which I will have more to say later on.

Flows: More Dif icult to Estimate Than Stocks Another important caveat concerns the income of nonwage workers, which may include remuneration 1 of capital that is difficult to distinguish from other income. To be sure, this problem is less important now than in the past because most private economic activity today is organized around corporations or, more generally, joint-stock companies, so a firm's accounts are clearly separate from the accounts of the individuals who supply the capital (who risk only the capital they have invested and not their personal fortunes, thanks to the revolutionary concept of the "limited liability corporation," which was adopted almost everywhere in the latter half of the nineteenth century). On the books of such a corporation, there is a clear distinction between remuneration of labor (wages, salaries, bonuses, and other payments to employees, including managers, who contribute labor to the company's activities) and remuneration of capital (dividends, interest, profits reinvested to increase the value of the firm's capital, etc.). Partnerships and sole proprietorships are different: the accounts of the business are sometimes mingled with the personal accounts of the firm head, who is often both the owner and operator. Today, around 10 percent of domestic production in the rich countries is due to nonwage workers in individually owned businesses, which is roughly equal to the proportion of nonwage workers in the active population. Nonwage workers are mostly found in small businesses (merchants, craftsmen, restaurant workers, etc.) and in the professions (doctors, lawyers, etc.). For a long time this category also included a large number of independent farmers, but today these have largely disappeared. On the books of these individually owned firms, it is generally impossible to distinguish the remuneration of capital: for example, the profits of a radiologist remunerate both her labor and the equipment she uses, which can be costly. The same is true of the hotel owner or small farmer. We therefore say that the income of nonwage workers is "mixed," because it combines income from labor with income from capital. This is also referred to as "entrepreneurial income." To apportion mixed incomes between capital and labor, I have used the same average capital-labor split as for the rest of the economy. This is the least arbitrary choice, and it appears to yield results close to those obtained with the other two commonly used methods. It remains an approximation, however, since the very notion of a clear boundary between income from capital and income fromlabor is not clearly defined for mixed incomes. For the current period, this makes virtually no difference: because the share of mixed income in national income is small, the uncertainty about capital's share of mixed income affects no more than 1–2 percent of national income. In earlier periods, and especially for the eighteenth and nineteenth centuries when mixed incomes may have accounted for more than half of national income, the uncertainties are potentially much greater. That is why available estimates of the capital share for the eighteenth and nineteenth centuries can only be counted as approximations. Despite these caveats, my estimates for capital's share of national income in this period (at least 40 percent) appear to be valid: in both Britain and France, the rents paid to landlords alone accounted for 20 percent of national income in the eighteenth and early nineteenth centuries, and all signs are that the return on farmland (which accounted for about half of national capital) was slightly less than the average return on capital and significantly less than the return on industrial capital, to judge by the very high level of industrial profits, especially during the first half of the nineteenth century. Because of imperfections in the available data, however, it is better to give an interval—between 35 and 40 percent—than a single estimate. 2 3 4 For the eighteenth and nineteenth centuries, estimates of the value of the capital stock are probably more accurate than estimates of the flows of income from labor and capital. This remains largely true today. That is why I chose to emphasize the evolution of the capital/income ratio rather than the capital-labor split, as most economic researchers have done in the past.

The principal conclusion that emerges from my estimates is the following. In both France and Britain, from the eighteenth century to the twenty-first, the pure return on capital has oscillated around a central value of 4–5 percent a year, or more generally in an interval from 3–6 percent a year. There has been no pronounced long-term trend either upward or downward. The pure return rose significantly above 6 percent following the massive destruction of property and numerous shocks to capital in the two world wars but subsequently returned fairly rapidly to the lower levels observed in the past. It is possible, however, that the pure return on capital has decreased slightly over the very long run: it often exceeded 4–5 percent in the eighteenth and nineteenth centuries, whereas in the early twenty-first century it seems to be approaching 3–4 percent as the capital/income ratio returns to the high levels observed in the past. We nevertheless lack the distance needed to be certain about this last point. We cannot rule out the possibility that the pure return on capital will rise to higher levels over the next few decades, especially in view of the growing international competition for capital and the equally increasing sophistication of financial markets and institutions in generating high yields from complex, diversified portfolios. In any case, this virtual stability of the pure return on capital over the very long run (or more likely this slight decrease of about one-quarter to one-fifth, from 4–5 percent in the eighteenth and nineteenth centuries to 3–4 percent today) is a fact of major importance for this study. In order to put these figures in perspective, recall first of all that the traditional rate of conversion from capital to rent in the eighteenth and nineteenth centuries, for the most common and least risky forms of capital (typically land and public debt) was generally on the order of 5 percent a year: the value of a capital asset was estimated to be equal to twenty years of the annual income yielded by that asset. Sometimes this was increased to twenty-five years (corresponding to a return of 4 percent a year). In classic novels of the early nineteenth century, such as those of Balzac and Jane Austen, the equivalence between capital and rent at a rate of 5 percent (or more rarely 4 percent) is taken for granted. Novelists frequently failed to mention the nature of the capital and generally treated land and public debt as almost perfect substitutes, mentioning only the yield in rent. We are told, for example, that a major character has 50,000 francs or 2,000 pounds sterling of rent but not whether it comes from land or from government bonds. It made no difference, since in both cases the income was certain and steady and sufficient to finance a very definite lifestyle and to reproduce across generations a familiar and well-understood social status. Similarly, neither Austen nor Balzac felt it necessary to specify the rate of return needed to transform a specific amount of capital into an annual rent: every reader knew full well that it took a capital on the order of 1 million francs to produce an annual rent of 50,000 francs (or a capital of 40,000 pounds to produce an income of 2,000 pounds a year), no matter whether the investment was in government bonds or land or something else entirely. For nineteenth-century novelists and their readers, the equivalence between wealth and annual rent was obvious, and there was no difficulty in moving from one measuring scale to the other, as if the two were perfectly synonymous. It was also obvious to novelists and their readers that some kinds of investment required greater 7 personal involvement, whether it was Père Goriot's pasta factories or Sir Thomas's plantations in the West Indies in Mansfield Park. What is more, the return on such investments was naturally higher, typically on the order of 7–8 percent or even more if one struck an especially good bargain, as César Birotteau hoped to do by investing in real estate in the Madeleine district of Paris after earlier successes in the perfume business. But it was also perfectly clear to everyone that when the time and energy devoted to organizing such affairs was deducted from the profits (think of the long months that Sir Thomas is forced to spend in the West Indies), the pure return obtained in the end was not always much more than the 4–5 percent earned by investments in land and government bonds. In other words, the additional yield was largely remuneration for the labor devoted to the business, and the pure return on capital, including the risk premium, was generally not much above 4–5 percent (which was not in any case a bad rate of return).

Too Much Capital Kills the Return on Capital Too much capital kills the return on capital: whatever the rules and institutions that structure the capital-labor split may be, it is natural to expect that the marginal productivity of capital decreases as the stock of capital increases. For example, if each agricultural worker already has thousands of hectares to farm, it is likely that the extra yield of an additional hectare of land will be limited. Similarly, if a country has already built a huge number of new dwellings, so that every resident enjoys hundreds of square feet of living space, then the increase to well-being of one additional building—as measured by the additional rent an individual would be prepared to pay in order to live in that building—would no doubt be very small. The same is true for machinery and equipment of any kind: marginal productivity decreases with quantity beyond a certain threshold. (Although it is possible that some minimum number of tools are needed to begin production, saturation is eventually reached.) Conversely, in a country where an enormous population must share a limited supply of land, scarce housing, and a small supply of tools, then the marginal product of an additional unit of capital will naturally be quite high, and the fortunate owners of that capital will not fail to take advantage of this. The interesting question is therefore not whether the marginal productivity of capital decreases when the stock of capital increases (this is obvious) but rather how fast it decreases. In particular, the central question is how much the return on capital r decreases (assuming that it is equal to the marginal productivity of capital) when the capital/income ratio β increases. Two cases are possible. If the return on capital r falls more than proportionately when the capital/ income ratio β increases (for example, if r decreases by more than half when β is doubled), then the share of capital income in national income $\alpha = r \times \beta$ decreases when β increases. In other words, the decrease in the return on capital more than compensates for the increase in the capital/ income ratio. Conversely, if the return r falls less than proportionately when β increases (for example, if r decreases by less than half when β is doubled), then capital's share $\alpha = r \times \beta$ increases when β increases. In that case, the effect of the decreased return on capital is simply to cushion and moderate the increase in the capital share compared to the increase in the capital/income ratio. 14 Based on historical evolutions observed in Britain and France, the second case seems more relevant over the long run: the capital share of income, α, follows the same U-shaped curve as the capital income ratio, β (with a high level in the eighteenth and nineteenth centuries, a drop in the middle of the twentieth century, and a rebound in the late twentieth and early twenty-first centuries). The evolution of the rate of return on capital, r, significantly reduces the amplitude of this U-curve, however: the return on capital was particularly high after World War II, when capital was scarce, in keeping with the principle of decreasing marginal productivity. But this effect was not strong enough to invert the U-curve of the capital/income ratio, β, and transform it into an inverted U-curve for the capital share α. It is nevertheless important to emphasize that both cases are theoretically possible. Everything depends on the vagaries of technology, or more precisely, everything depends on the range of technologies available to combine capital and labor to produce the various types of goods and services that society wants to consume. In thinking about these questions, economists often use the concept of a "production function," which is a mathematical formula reflecting the technological possibilities that exist in a given society. One characteristic of a production function is that it defines an elasticity of substitution between capital and labor: that is, it measures how easy it is to substitute capital for labor, or labor for capital, to produce required goods and services. For example, if the coefficients of the production function are completely fixed, then the elasticity of substitution is zero: it takes exactly one hectare and one tool per agricultural worker (or one machine per industrial worker), neither more nor less. If each worker has as little as 1/100 hectare too much or one tool too many, the marginal productivity of the additional capital will be zero. Similarly, if the number of workers is one too many for the available capital stock, the extra worker cannot be put to work in any productive way. Conversely, if the elasticity of substitution is infinite, the marginal productivity of capital (and labor) is totally independent of the available quantity of capital and labor. In particular, the return on capital is fixed and does not depend on the quantity of capital: it is always possible to accumulate more capital and increase production by a fixed percentage, for example, 5 or 10 percent a year per unit of additional capital. Think of an entirely robotized economy in which one can increase production at will simply by adding more capital. Neither of these two extreme cases is really relevant: the first sins by want of imagination and the second by excess of technological optimism (or pessimism about the human race, depending on one's point of view). The relevant question is whether the elasticity of substitution between labor and capital is greater or less than one. If the elasticity lies between zero and one, then an increase in the capital/income ratio β leads to a decrease in the marginal productivity of capital large enough that the capital share $\alpha = r \times \beta$ decreases (assuming that the return on capital is determined by its marginal productivity). If the elasticity is greater than one, an increase in the capital/income ratio β leads instead to a drop in the marginal productivity of capital, so that the capital share $\alpha = r \times \beta$ increases (again assuming that the return on capital is equal to its marginal productivity). If the elasticity is exactly equal to one, then the two effects cancel each other out: the return on capital decreases in exactly the same proportion as the capital/income ratio β increases, so that the product $\alpha = r \times \beta$ does not change. 15 16 Beyond Cobb-Douglas: The Question of the Stability of the Capital-Labor Split The case of an elasticity of substitution exactly equal to one corresponds to the so-called CobbDouglas production function, named for the economists Charles Cobb and Paul Douglas, who first proposed it in 1928. With a Cobb-Douglas production function, no matter what happens, and in particular no matter what quantities of capital and labor are available, the capital share of income is always equal to the fixed coefficient α, which can be taken as a purely technological parameter. For example, if $\alpha = 30$ percent, then no matter what the capital/income ratio is, income from capital will account for 30 percent of national income (and income from labor for 70 percent). If the savings rate and growth rate are such that the long-term capital/income ratio $\beta = s / g$ corresponds to six years of national income, then the rate of return on capital will be 5 percent, so that the capital share of income will be 30 percent. If the long-term capital stock is only three years of national income, then the return on capital will rise to 10 percent. And if the savings and growth rates are such that the capital stock represents ten years of national income, then the return on capital will fall to 3 percent. In all cases, the capital share of income will be 30 percent. The Cobb-Douglas production function became very popular in economics textbooks after World War II (after being popularized by Paul Samuelson), in part for good reasons but also in part for bad ones, including simplicity (economists like simple stories, even when they are only approximately correct), but above all because the stability of the capital-labor split gives a fairly peaceful and harmonious view of the social order. In fact, the stability of capital's share of income—assuming it turns out to be true—in no way guarantees harmony: it is compatible with extreme and untenable inequality of the ownership of capital and distribution of income. Contrary to a widespread idea, moreover, stability of capital's share of national income in no way implies stability of the capital/income ratio, which can easily take on very different values at different times and in different countries, so that, in particular, there can be substantial international imbalances in the ownership of capital. The point I want to emphasize, however, is that historical reality is more complex than the idea of a completely stable capital-labor split suggests. The Cobb-Douglas hypothesis is sometimes a good approximation for certain subperiods or sectors and, in any case, is a useful point of departure for further reflection. But this hypothesis does not satisfactorily explain the diversity of the historical patterns we observe over the long, short, or medium run, as the data I have collected show. Furthermore, there is nothing really surprising about this, given that economists had very little historical data to go on when Cobb and Douglas first proposed their hypothesis. In their original article, published in 1928, these two American economists used data about US manufacturing in the period 1899–1922, which did indeed show a certain stability in the share of income going to profits. This idea appears to have been first introduced by the British economist Arthur Bowley, who in 1920 published an important book on the distribution of British national income in the period 1880–1913 whose primary conclusion was that the capital-labor split remained relatively stable during this period. Clearly, however, the periods analyzed by these authors were relatively short: in particular, they did not try to compare their results with estimates from the early nineteenth century (much less the eighteenth). As noted, moreover, these questions aroused very strong political tensions in the late nineteenth and 17 18 19 early twentieth centuries, as well as throughout the Cold War, that were not conducive to a calmconsideration of the facts. Both conservative and liberal economists were keen to show that growth benefited everyone and thus were very attached to the idea that the capital-labor split was perfectly stable, even if believing this sometimes meant neglecting data or periods that suggested an increase in the share of income going to capital. By the same token, Marxist economists liked to show that capital's share was always increasing while wages stagnated, even if believing this sometimes required twisting the data. In 1899, Eduard Bernstein, who had the temerity to argue that wages were increasing and the working class had much to gain from collaborating with the existing regime (he was even prepared to become vice president of the Reichstag), was roundly outvoted at the congress of the German Social Democratic Party in Hanover. In 1937, the young German historian and economist Jürgen Kuczynski, who later became a well-known professor of economic history at Humboldt

University in East Berlin and who in 1960–1972 published a monumental thirty-eightvolume universal history of wages, attacked Bowley and other bourgeois economists. Kuczynski argued that labor's share of national income had decreased steadily from the advent of industrial capitalism until the 1930s. This was true for the first half—indeed, the first two-thirds—of the nineteenth century but wrong for the entire period. In the years that followed, controversy raged in the pages of academic journals. In 1939, in Economic History Review, where calmer debates where the norm, Frederick Brown unequivocally backed Bowley, whom he characterized as a "great scholar" and "serious statistician," whereas Kuczynski in his view was nothing more than a "manipulator," a charge that was wide of the mark. Also in 1939, Keynes took the side of the bourgeois economists, calling the stability of the capital-labor split "one of the best-established regularities in all of economic science." This assertion was hasty to say the least, since Keynes was essentially relying on data from British manufacturing industry in the 1920s, which were insufficient to establish a universal regularity. In textbooks published in the period 1950–1970 (and indeed as late as 1990), a stable capital-labor split is generally presented as an uncontroversial fact, but unfortunately the period to which this supposed law applies is not always clearly specified. Most authors are content to use data going back no further than 1950, avoiding comparison with the interwar period or the early twentieth century, much less with the eighteenth and nineteenth centuries. From the 1990s on, however, numerous studies mention a significant increase in the share of national income in the rich countries going to profits and capital after 1970, along with the concomitant decrease in the share going to wages and labor. The universal stability thesis thus began to be questioned, and in the 2000s several official reports published by the Organisation for Economic Cooperation and Development (OECD) and International Monetary Fund (IMF) took note of the phenomenon (a sign that the question was being taken seriously). The novelty of this study is that it is to my knowledge the first attempt to place the question of the capital-labor split and the recent increase of capital's share of national income in a broader historical context by focusing on the evolution of the capital/income ratio from the eighteenth century until now. The exercise admittedly has its limits, in view of the imperfections of the available historical sources, but I believe that it gives us a better view of the major issues and puts the question in a whole new light. 20 21 22 23 Capital-Labor Substitution in the Twenty-First Century: An Elasticity Greater Than

One I begin by examining the inadequacy of the Cobb-Douglas model for studying evolutions over the very long run. Over a very long period of time, the elasticity of substitution between capital and labor seems to have been greater than one: an increase in the capital/income ratio β seems to have led to a slight increase in α, capital's share of national income, and vice versa. Intuitively, this corresponds to a situation in which there are many different uses for capital in the long run. Indeed, the observed historical evolutions suggest that it is always possible—up to a certain point, at least—to find new and useful things to do with capital: for example, new ways of building and equipping houses (think of solar panels on rooftops or digital lighting controls), ever more sophisticated robots and other electronic devices, and medical technologies requiring larger and larger capital investments. One need not imagine a fully robotized economy in which capital would reproduce itself (corresponding to an infinite elasticity of substitution) to appreciate the many uses of capital in a diversified advanced economy in which the elasticity of substitution is greater than one. It is obviously quite difficult to predict how much greater than one the elasticity of substitution of capital for labor will be in the twenty-first century. On the basis of historical data, one can estimate an elasticity between 1.3 and 1.6. But not only is this estimate uncertain and imprecise. More than that, there is no reason why the technologies of the future should exhibit the same elasticity as those of the past. The only thing that appears to be relatively well established is that the tendency for the capital/income ratio β to rise, as has been observed in the rich countries in recent decades and might spread to other countries around the world if growth (and especially demographic growth) slows in the twenty-first century, may well be accompanied by a durable increase in capital's share of national income, α. To be sure, it is likely that the return on capital, r, will decrease as β increases. But on the basis of historical experience, the most likely outcome is that the volume effect will outweigh the price effect, which means that the accumulation effect will outweigh the decrease in the return on capital. Indeed, the available data indicate that capital's share of income increased in most rich countries between 1970 and 2010 to the extent that the capital/income ratio increased Note, however, that this upward trend is consistent not only with an elasticity of substitution greater than one but also with an increase in capital's bargaining power vis-à-vis labor over the past few decades, which have seen increased mobility of capital and heightened competition between states eager to attract investments. It is likely that the two effects have reinforced each other in recent years, and it is also possible that this will continue to be the case in the future. In any event, it is important to point out that no self-corrective mechanism exists to prevent a steady increase of the capital/income ratio, β, together with a steady rise in capital's share of national income, α.

Traditional Agricultural Societies: An Elasticity Less Than One I have just shown that an important characteristic of contemporary economies is the existence of many opportunities to substitute capital for labor. It is interesting that this was not at all the case in traditional economies based on agriculture, where capital existed mainly in the form of land. The available historical data suggest very clearly that the elasticity of substitution was significantly less than one in traditional agricultural societies. In particular, this is the only way to explain why, in the eighteenth and nineteenth centuries, the value of land in the United States, as measured by the capital/income ratio and land rents, was much lower than in Europe, even though land was much more plentiful in the New World. This is perfectly logical, moreover: if capital is to serve as a ready substitute for labor, then it must exist in different forms. For any given form of capital (such as farmland in the case in point), it is inevitable that beyond a certain point, the price effect will outweigh the volume effect. If a few hundred individuals have an entire continent at their disposal, then it stands to reason that the price of land and land rents will fall to near-zero levels. There is no better illustration of the maxim "Too much capital kills the return on capital" than the relative value of land and land rents in the New World and the Old. Is Human Capital Illusory? The time has come to turn to a very important question: Has the apparently growing importance of human capital over the course of history been an illusion? Let me rephrase the question in more precise terms. Many people believe that what characterizes the process of development and economic growth is the increased importance of human labor, skill, and know-how in the production process. Although this hypothesis is not always formulated in explicit terms, one reasonable interpretation would be that technology has changed in such a way that the labor factor now plays a greater role. Indeed, it seems plausible to interpret in this way the decrease in capital's share of income over the very long run, from 35–40 percent in 1800–1810 to 25–30 percent in 2000–2010, with a 25 corresponding increase in labor's share from 60–65 percent to 70–75 percent. Labor's share increased simply because labor became more important in the production process. Thus it was the growing power of human capital that made it possible to decrease the share of income going to land, buildings, and financial capital. If this interpretation is correct, then the transformation to which it points was indeed quite significant. Caution is in order, however. For one thing, as noted earlier, we do not have sufficient perspective at this point in history to reach an adequate judgment about the very long-run evolution of capital's share of income. It is quite possible that capital's share will increase in coming decades to the level it reached at the beginning of the nineteenth century. This may happen even if the structural form of technology—and the relative importance of capital and labor—does not change (although the relative bargaining power of labor and capital may change) or if technology changes only slightly (which seems to me the more plausible alternative) yet the increase in the capital/income ratio drives capital's share of income toward or perhaps beyond historic peaks because the long-run elasticity of substitution of capital for labor is apparently greater than one. This is perhaps the most important lesson of this study thus far: modern technology still uses a great deal of capital, and even more important, because capital has many uses, one can accumulate enormous amounts of it without reducing its return to zero. Under these conditions, there is no reason why capital's share must decrease over the very long run, even if technology changes in a way that is relatively favorable to labor. A second reason for caution is the following. The probable long-run decrease in capital's share of national income from 35–40 percent to 25–30 percent is, I think, quite plausible and surely significant but does not amount to a change of civilization. Clearly, skill levels have increased markedly over the past two centuries. But the stock of industrial, financial, and real estate capital has also increased enormously. Some people think that capital has lost its importance and that we have magically gone from a civilization based on capital, inheritance, and kinship to one based on human capital and talent. Fat-cat stockholders have supposedly been replaced by talented managers thanks solely to changes in technology. I will come back to this question in Part Three when I turn to the study of individual inequalities in the distribution of income and wealth: a correct answer at this stage is impossible. But I have already shown enough to warn against such mindless optimism: capital has not disappeared for the simple reason that it is still useful—hardly less useful than in the era of Balzac and Austen, perhaps—and may well remain so in the future. Medium-Term Changes in the Capital-Labor Split I have just shown that the Cobb-Douglas hypothesis of a completely stable capital-labor split cannot give a totally satisfactory explanation of the long-term evolution of the capital-labor split. The same can be said, perhaps even more strongly, about short- and medium-term evolutions, which can in some cases extend over fairly long periods, particularly as seen by contemporary witnesses to these changes. The most important case, which I discussed briefly in the Introduction, is no doubt the increase in capital's share of income during the early phases of the Industrial Revolution, from 1800 to 1860. In Britain, for which we have the most complete data, the available historical studies, in particular those of Robert Allen (who gave the name "Engels' pause" to the long stagnation of wages), suggest that capital's share increased by something like 10 percent of national income, from 35–40 percent in the late eighteenth and early nineteenth centuries to around 45–50 percent in the middle of the nineteenth century, when Marx wrote The Communist Manifesto and set to work on Capital. The sources also suggest that this increase was roughly compensated by a comparable decrease in capital's share in the period 1870–1900, followed by a slight increase between 1900 and 1910, so that in the end the capital share was probably not very different around the turn of the twentieth century from what it was during the French Revolution and Napoleonic era (see Figure 6.1). We can therefore speak of a "medium-term" movement rather than a durable long-term trend. Nevertheless, this transfer of 10 percent of national income to capital during the first half of the nineteenth century was by no means negligible: to put it in concrete terms, the lion's share of economic growth in this period went to profits, while wages—objectively miserable—stagnated. According to Allen, the main explanation for this was the exodus of labor from the countryside and into the cities, together with technological changes that increased the productivity of capital (reflected by a structural change in the production function)—the caprices of technology, in short. Available historical data for France suggest a similar chronology. In particular, all the sources indicate a serious stagnation of wages in the period 1810–1850 despite robust industrial growth. The data collected by Jean Bouvier and François Furet from the books of leading French industrial firms confirm this chronology: the share of profits increased until 1860, then decreased from 1870 to 1900, and rose again between 1900 and 1910. The data we have for the eighteenth century and the period of the French Revolution also suggest an increase in the share of income going to land rent in the decades preceding the revolution (which seems consistent with Arthur Young's observations about the misery of French peasants), and substantial wage increases between 1789 and 1815 (which can conceivably be explained by the redistribution of land and the mobilization of labor to meet the needs of military conflict). When the lower classes of the Restoration and July Monarchy looked back on the revolutionary period and the Napoleonic era, they accordingly remembered good times. To remind ourselves that these short- and medium-term changes in the capital-labor split occur at many different times, I have shown the annual evolution in France from 1900 to 2010 in Figures 6.6–8, in which I distinguish the evolution of the wage-profit split in value added by firms from the evolution of the share of rent in national income. Note, in particular, that the wage-profit split has gone through three distinct phases since World War II, with a sharp rise in profits from 1945 to 1968 followed by a very pronounced drop in the share of profits from 1968 to 1983 and then a very rapid rise after 1983 leading to stabilization in the early 1990s. I will have more to say about this highly political chronology in subsequent chapters, where I will discuss the dynamics of income inequality. Note the steady rise of the share of national income going to rent since 1945, which implies that the share going to capital overall continued to increase between 1990 and 2010, despite the stabilization of the profit share.

Back to Marx and the Falling Rate of Profit As I come to the end of this examination of the historical dynamics of the capital/income ratio and the capital-labor split, it is worth pointing out the relation between my conclusions and the theses of Karl Marx. For Marx, the central mechanism by which "the bourgeoisie digs its own grave" corresponded to what I referred to in the Introduction as "the principle of infinite accumulation": capitalists accumulate ever increasing quantities of capital, which ultimately leads inexorably to a falling rate of profit (i.e., return on capital) and eventually to their own downfall. Marx did not use mathematical models, and his prose was not always limpid, so it is difficult to be sure what he had in mind. But one logically consistent way of interpreting his thought is to consider the dynamic law $\beta = s / g$ in the special case where the growth rate g is zero or very close to zero. Recall that g measures the long-term structural growth rate, which is the sum of productivity growth and population growth. In Marx's mind, as in the minds of all nineteenth- and early twentieth-century economists before Robert Solow did his work on growth in the 1950s, the very idea of structural growth, driven by permanent and durable growth of productivity, was not clearly identified or formulated. In those days, the implicit hypothesis was that growth of production, and especially of manufacturing output, was explained mainly by the accumulation of industrial capital. In other words, output increased solely because every worker was backed by more machinery and equipment and not because productivity as such (for a given quantity of labor and capital) increased. Today we know that long-term structural growth is possible only because of productivity growth. But this was not obvious in Marx's time, owing to lack of historical perspective and good data. Where there is no structural growth, and the productivity and population growth rate g is zero, we run up against a logical contradiction very close to what Marx described. If the savings rate s is positive, meaning the capitalists insist on accumulating more and more capital every year in order to increase their power and perpetuate their advantages or simply because their standard of living is already so high, then the capital/income ratio will increase indefinitely. More generally, if g is close to zero, the long-term capital/income ratio $\beta = s / g$ tends toward infinity. And if β is extremely large, then the return on capital r must get smaller and smaller and closer and closer to zero, or else capital's share of income, $\alpha = r \times \beta$, will ultimately devour all of national income. The dynamic inconsistency that Marx pointed out thus corresponds to a real difficulty, from which the only logical exit is structural growth, which is the only way of balancing the process of capital accumulation (to a certain extent). Only permanent growth of productivity and population can compensate for the permanent addition of new units of capital, as the law $\beta = s / g$ makes clear. Otherwise, capitalists do indeed dig their own grave: either they tear each other apart in a desperate attempt to combat the falling rate of profit (for instance, by waging war over the best colonial investments, as Germany and France did in the Moroccan crises of 1905 and 1911), or they force labor to accept a smaller and smaller share of national income, which ultimately leads to a proletarian revolution and general expropriation. In any event, capital is undermined by its internal contradictions. That Marx actually had a model of this kind in mind (i.e., a model based on infinite accumulation of capital) is confirmed by his use on several occasions of the account books of industrial firms with very high capital intensities. In volume 1 of Capital, for instance, he uses the books of a textile factory, which were conveyed to him, he says, "by the owner," and seem to show an extremely high 31 32 ratio of the total amount of fixed and variable capital used in the production process to the value of a year's output—apparently greater than ten. A capital/

income ratio of this level is indeed rather frightening. If the rate of return on capital is 5 percent, then more than half the value of the firm's output goes to profits. It was natural for Marx and many other anxious contemporary observers to ask where all this might lead (especially because wages had been stagnant since the beginning of the nineteenth century) and what type of long-run socioeconomic equilibrium such hyper-capital-intensive industrial development would produce. Marx was also an assiduous reader of British parliamentary reports from the period 1820–1860. He used these reports to document the misery of wage workers, workplace accidents, deplorable health conditions, and more generally the rapacity of the owners of industrial capital. He also used statistics derived from taxes imposed on profits from different sources, which showed a very rapid increase of industrial profits in Britain during the 1840s. Marx even tried—in a very impressionistic fashion, to be sure—to make use of probate statistics in order to show that the largest British fortunes had increased dramatically since the Napoleonic wars. The problem is that despite these important intuitions, Marx usually adopted a fairly anecdotal and unsystematic approach to the available statistics. In particular, he did not try to find out whether the very high capital intensity that he observed in the account books of certain factories was representative of the British economy as a whole or even of some particular sector of the economy, as he might have done by collecting just a few dozen similar accounts. The most surprising thing, given that his book was devoted largely to the question of capital accumulation, is that he makes no reference to the numerous attempts to estimate the British capital stock that had been carried out since the beginning of the eighteenth century and extended in the nineteenth century by work beginning with Patrick Colqhoun between 1800 and 1810 and continuing through Giffen in the 1870s. Marx seems to have missed entirely the work on national accounting that was developing around him, and this is all the more unfortunate in that it would have enabled him to some extent to confirm his intuitions concerning the vast accumulation of private capital in this period and above all to clarify his explanatory model. Beyond the "Two Cambridges" It is important to recognize, however, that the national accounts and other statistical data available in the late nineteenth and early twentieth centuries were wholly inadequate for a correct understanding of the dynamics of the capital/income ratio. In particular, there were many more estimates of the stock of national capital than of national income or domestic product. By the mid-twentieth century, following the shocks of

1914–1945, the reverse was true. This no doubt explains why the question of capital accumulation and a possible dynamic equilibrium continued to stir controversy and arouse a good deal of confusion for so long. A good example of this is the famous "Cambridge capital controversy" of the 1950s and 1960s (also called the "Two Cambridges Debate" because it pitted Cambridge, England, against Cambridge, Massachusetts). To briefly recall the main points of this debate: when the formula $\beta = s\,/\,g$ was explicitly introduced for the first time by the economists Roy Harrod and Evsey Domar in the late 1930s, it was common to invert it as $g = s\,/\,\beta$. Harrod, in particular, argued in 1939 that β was fixed by the 33 34 available technology (as in the case of a production function with fixed coefficients and no possible substitution between labor and capital), so that the growth rate was entirely determined by the savings rate. If the savings rate is 10 percent and technology imposes a capital/income ratio of 5 (so that it takes exactly five units of capital, neither more nor less, to produce one unit of output), then the growth rate of the economy's productive capacity is 2 percent per year. But since the growth rate must also be equal to the growth rate of the population (and of productivity, which at the time was still ill defined), it follows that growth is an intrinsically unstable process, balanced "on a razor's edge." There is always either too much or too little capital, which therefore gives rise either to excess capacity and speculative bubbles or else to unemployment, or perhaps both at once, depending on the sector and the year. Harrod's intuition was not entirely wrong, and he was writing in the midst of the Great Depression, an obvious sign of great macroeconomic instability. Indeed, the mechanism he described surely helps to explain why the growth process is always highly volatile: to bring savings into line with investment at the national level, when savings and investment decisions are generally made by different individuals for different reasons, is a structurally complex and chaotic phenomenon, especially since it is often difficult in the short run to alter the capital intensity and organization of production. Nevertheless, the capital/income ratio is relatively flexible in the long run, as is unambiguously demonstrated by the very large historical variations that are observed in the data, together with the fact that the elasticity of substitution of capital for labor has apparently been greater than one over a long period of time. In 1948, Domar developed a more optimistic and flexible version of the law $g = s\,/\,\beta$ than Harrod's. Domar stressed the fact that the savings rate and capital/income ratio can to a certain extent adjust to each other. Even more important was Solow's introduction in 1956 of a production function with substitutable factors, which made it possible to invert the formula and write $\beta = s \, / \, g$. In the long run, the capital/income ratio adjusts to the savings rate and structural growth rate of the economy rather than the other way around. Controversy continued, however, in the 1950s and 1960s between economists based primarily in Cambridge, Massachusetts (including Solow and Samuelson, who defended the production function with substitutable factors) and economists working in Cambridge, England (including Joan Robinson, Nicholas Kaldor, and Luigi Pasinetti), who (not without a certain confusion at times) saw in Solow's model a claim that growth is always perfectly balanced, thus negating the importance Keynes had attributed to short-term fluctuations. It was not until the 1970s that Solow's so-called neoclassical growth model definitively carried the day. If one rereads the exchanges in this controversy with the benefit of hindsight, it is clear that the debate, which at times had a marked postcolonial dimension (as American economists sought to emancipate themselves from the historic tutelage of their British counterparts, who had reigned over the profession since the time of Adam Smith, while the British sought to defend the memory of Lord Keynes, which they thought the American economists had betrayed), did more to cloud economic thinking than to enlighten it. There was no real justification for the suspicions of the British. Solow and Samuelson were fully convinced that the growth process is unstable in the short term and that macroeconomic stabilization requires Keynesian policies, and they viewed $\beta = s \, / \, g$ solely as a longterm law. Nevertheless, the American economists, some of whom (for example Franco Modigliani) 35 were born in Europe, tended at times to exaggerate the implications of the "balanced growth path" they had discovered. To be sure, the law $\beta = s \, / \, g$ describes a growth path in which all macroeconomic quantities—capital stock, income and output flows—progress at the same pace over the long run. Still, apart from the question of short-term volatility, such balanced growth does not guarantee a harmonious distribution of wealth and in no way implies the disappearance or even reduction of inequality in the ownership of capital. Furthermore, contrary to an idea that until recently was widespread, the law $\beta = s \, / \, g$ in no way precludes very large variations in the capital/income ratio over time and between countries. Quite the contrary. In my view, the virulence—and at times sterility—of the Cambridge capital controversy was due in part to the fact that participants on both sides lacked the historical data needed to clarify the terms of the debate. It is striking to see how little use either side made of national capital estimates done prior to World War I; they probably believed them to be incompatible with the realities of the 1950s and 1960s. The two world wars created such a deep discontinuity in both conceptual and statistical analysis that for a while it seemed impossible to study the issue in a long-run perspective, especially from a European point of view. Capital's Comeback in a Low-Growth Regime The truth is that only since the end of the twentieth century have we had the statistical data and above all the indispensable historical distance to correctly analyze the long-run dynamics of the capital/income ratio and the capital-labor split. Specifically, the data I have assembled and the historical distance we are fortunate enough to enjoy (still insufficient, to be sure, but by definition greater than that which previous authors had) lead to the following conclusions. First, the return to a historic regime of low growth, and in particular zero or even negative demographic growth, leads logically to the return of capital. This tendency for low-growth societies to reconstitute very large stocks of capital is expressed by the law $\beta = s\,/\,g$ and can be summarized as follows: in stagnant societies, wealth accumulated in the past naturally takes on considerable importance. In Europe today, the capital/income ratio has already risen to around five to six years of national income, scarcely less than the level observed in the eighteenth and nineteenth centuries and up to the eve of World War I. At the global level, it is entirely possible that the capital/income ratio will attain or even surpass this level during the twenty-first century. If the savings rate is now around 10 percent and the growth rate stabilizes at around 1.5 percent in the very long run, then the global stock of capital will logically rise to six or seven years of income. And if growth falls to 1 percent, the capital stock could rise as high as ten years of income. As for capital's share in national and global income, which is given by the law $\alpha = r \times \beta$, experience suggests that the predictable rise in the capital/income ratio will not necessarily lead to a significant drop in the return on capital. There are many uses for capital over the very long run, and this fact can be captured by noting that the long-run elasticity of substitution of capital for labor is probably greater than one. The most likely outcome is thus that the decrease in the rate of return will be smaller than the increase in the capital/income ratio, so that capital's share will increase. With a capital/income ratio of seven to eight years and a rate of return on capital of 4–5 percent, capital's 36 share of global income could amount to 30 or 40 percent, a level close to that observed in theeighteenth and nineteenth centuries, and it might rise even higher. As noted, it is also possible that technological changes over the very long run will slightly favorhuman labor over capital, thus lowering the return on capital and the capital share. But the size of thislong-term effect seems limited, and it is possible that it will be more than compensated by otherforces tending in the opposite direction, such as the creation of increasingly sophisticated systems offinancial intermediation and international competition for capital. The Caprices of Technology The principal lesson of this second part of the book is surely that there is no natural force thatinevitably reduces the importance of capital and of income flowing from ownership of capital overthe course of history. In the decades after World War II, people began to think that the triumph ofhuman capital over capital in the traditional sense (land, buildings, and financial capital) was anatural and irreversible process, due perhaps to technology and to purely economic forces. In fact,however, some people were already saying that political forces were central. My results fullyconfirm this view. Progress toward economic and technological rationality need not imply progresstoward democratic and meritocratic rationality. The primary reason for this is simple: technology,like the market, has neither limits nor morality. The evolution of technology has certainly increasedthe need for human skills and competence. But it has also increased the need for buildings, homes,offices, equipment of all kinds, patents, and so on, so that in the end the total value of all these formsof nonhuman capital (real estate, business capital, industrial capital, financial capital) has increasedalmost as rapidly as total income from labor. If one truly wishes to found a more just and rationalsocial order based on common utility, it is not enough to count on the caprices of technology. To sum up: modern growth, which is based on the growth of productivity and the diffusion ofknowledge, has made it possible to avoid the apocalypse predicted by Marx and to balance theprocess of capital accumulation. But it has not altered the deep structures of capital—or at any ratehas not truly reduced the macroeconomic importance of capital relative to labor. I must now examinewhether the same is true for inequality in the distribution of income and wealth. How much has thestructure of inequality with respect to both labor and capital actually changed since the nineteenth century?

CHAPTER SEVEN

Inequality and Concentration: Preliminary Bearings

Balzac's Père Goriot, published in 1835, could not be clearer. Père Goriot, a former spaghetti maker, has made a fortune in pasta and grain during the Revolution and Napoleonic era. A widower, he sacrifices everything he has to find husbands for his daughters Delphine and Anastasie in the best Parisian society of the 1810s. He keeps just enough to pay his room and board in a shabby boardinghouse, where he meets Eugène de Rastignac, a penniless young noble who has come up fromthe provinces to study law in Paris. Full of ambition and humiliated by his poverty, Eugène avails himself of the help of a distant cousin to worm his way into the luxurious salons where the aristocracy, grande bourgeoisie, and high finance of the Restoration mingle. He quickly falls in love with Delphine, who has been abandoned by her husband, Baron de Nucingen, a banker who has already used his wife's dowry in any number of speculative ventures. Rastignac soon sheds his illusions as he discovers the cynicism of a society entirely corrupted by money. He is appalled to learn how Père Goriot has been abandoned by his daughters, who, preoccupied as they are with social success, are ashamed of their father and have seen little of him since availing themselves of his fortune. The old man dies in sordid poverty and solitude. Only Rastignac attends his burial. But no sooner has he left Père Lachaise cemetery than he is overwhelmed by the sight of Parisian wealth on display along the Seine and decides to set out in conquest of the capital: "It's just you and me now!" he apostrophizes the city. His sentimental and social education is over. From this point on he, too, will be ruthless. The darkest moment in the novel, when the social and moral dilemmas Rastignac faces are rawest and clearest, comes at the midpoint, when the shady character Vautrin offers him a lesson about his future prospects. Vautrin, who resides in the same shabby boardinghouse as Rastignac and Goriot, is a glib talker and seducer who is concealing a dark past as a convict, much like Edmond Dantès in Le Comte de Monte-Cristo or Jean Valjean in Les Misérables. In contrast to those two characters, who are on the whole worthy fellows, Vautrin is deeply wicked and cynical. He attempts to lure Rastignac into committing a murder in order to lay hands on a large legacy. Before that, Vautrin offers Rastignac an extremely lurid, detailed lesson about the different fates that might befall a young man in the French society of the day. In substance, Vautrin explains to Rastignac that it is illusory to think that social success can be achieved through study, talent, and effort. He paints a detailed portrait of the various possible careers that await his young friend if he pursues studies in law or medicine, fields in which professional competence counts more than inherited wealth. In particular, Vautrin explains very clearly to Rastignac what yearly income he can aspire to in each of these professions. The verdict is clear: even if he ranks at the top of his class and quickly achieves a brilliant career in law, which will require many compromises, he will still have to get by on a mediocre income and give up all hope of becoming truly wealthy: By the age of thirty, you will be a judge making 1,200 francs a year, if you haven't yet tossed away your robes. When you reach forty, you will marry a miller's daughter with an income of around 6,000 livres. Thank you very much. If you're lucky enough to find a patron, you will become a royal prosecutor at thirty, with compensation of a thousand écus [5,000 francs], and you will marry the mayor's daughter. If you're willing to do a little political dirty work, you will be a prosecutor-general by the time you're forty.... It is my privilege to point out to you, however, that there are only twenty prosecutors-general in France, while 20,000 of you aspire to the position, and among them are a few clowns who would sell their families to move up a rung. If this profession disgusts you, consider another. Would Baron de Rastignac like to be a 1 lawyer? Very well then! You will need to suffer ten years of misery, spend a thousand francs a month, acquire a library and an office, frequent society, kiss the hem of a clerk to get cases, and lick the courthouse floor with your tongue. If the profession led anywhere, I wouldn't advise you against it. But can you name five lawyers in Paris who earn more than 50,000 francs a year at the age of fifty? By contrast, the strategy for social success that Vautrin proposes to Rastignac is quite a bit more efficient. By marrying Mademoiselle Victorine, a shy young woman who lives in the boardinghouse and has eyes only for the handsome Eugène, he will immediately lay hands on a fortune of a million francs. This will enable him to draw at age twenty an annual income of 50,000 francs (5 percent of the capital) and thus immediately achieve ten times the level of comfort to which he could hope to aspire only years later on a royal prosecutor's salary (and as much as the most prosperous Parisian lawyers of the day earned at age fifty after years of effort and intrigue). The conclusion is clear: he must lose no time in marrying young Victorine, ignoring the fact that she is neither very pretty nor very appealing. Eugène eagerly heeds Vautrin's lesson right up to the ultimate coup de grâce: if the illegitimate child Victorine is to be recognized by her wealthy father and become the heiress of the million francs Vautrin has mentioned, her brother must first be killed. The ex-convict is ready to take on this task in exchange for a commission. This is too much for Rastignac: although he is quite amenable to Vautrin's arguments concerning the merits of inheritance over study, he is not prepared to commit murder. The Key Question: Work or Inheritance? What is most frightening about Vautrin's lecture is that his brisk portrait of Restoration society contains such precise figures. As I will soon show, the structure of the income and wealth hierarchies in nineteenth-century France was such that the standard of living the wealthiest French people could attain greatly exceeded that to which one could aspire on the basis of income from labor alone. Under such conditions, why work? And why behave morally at all? Since social inequality was in itself immoral and unjustified, why not be thoroughly immoral and appropriate capital by whatever means are available? The detailed income figures Vautrin gives are unimportant (although quite realistic): the key fact is that in nineteenth-century France and, for that matter, into the early twentieth century, work and study alone were not enough to achieve the same level of comfort afforded by inherited wealth and the income derived from it. This was so obvious to everyone that Balzac needed no statistics to prove it, no detailed figures concerning the deciles and centiles of the income hierarchy. Conditions were similar, moreover, in eighteenth- and nineteenth-century Britain. For Jane Austen's heroes, the question of work did not arise: all that mattered was the size of one's fortune, whether acquired through inheritance or marriage. Indeed, the same was true almost everywhere before World War I, which marked the suicide of the patrimonial societies of the past. One of the few exceptions to this rule was the United States, or at any rate the various "pioneer" microsocieties in the northern and western states, where inherited capital had little influence in the eighteenth and nineteenth centuries—a situation that did not last long, however. In the southern states, where capital in the form of slaves 2 and land predominated, inherited wealth mattered as much as it did in old Europe. In Gone with the Wind, Scarlett O'Hara's suitors cannot count on their studies or talents to assure their future comfort any more than Rastignac can: the size of one's father's (or father-in-law's) plantation matters far more. Vautrin, to show how little he thinks of morality, merit, or social justice, points out to young Eugène that he would be glad to end his days as a slave owner in the US South, living in opulence on what his Negroes produced. Clearly, the America that appeals to the French ex-convict is not the America that appealed to Tocqueville. To be sure, income from labor is not always equitably distributed, and it would be unfair to reduce the question of social justice to the importance of income from labor versus income from inherited wealth. Nevertheless, democratic modernity is founded on the belief that inequalities based on individual talent and effort are more justified than other inequalities—or at any rate we hope to be moving in that direction. Indeed, Vautrin's lesson to some extent ceased to be valid in twentiethcentury Europe, at least for a time. During the decades that followed World War II, inherited wealth lost much of its importance, and for the first time in history, perhaps, work and study became the surest routes to the top. Today, even though all sorts of inequalities have reemerged, and many beliefs in social and democratic progress have been shaken, most people still believe that the world has changed radically since Vautrin lectured Rastignac. Who today would advise a young law student to abandon his or her studies and adopt the ex-convict's strategy for social advancement? To be sure, there may exist rare cases where a person would be well advised to set his or her sights on inheriting a large fortune. In the vast majority of cases, however, it is not only more moral but also more profitable to rely on study, work, and professional success. Vautrin's lecture focuses our attention on two questions, which I will try to answer in the next few chapters with the imperfect data at my disposal. First, can we be sure that the relative importance of income from labor versus income from inherited wealth has been transformed since the time of Vautrin, and if so, to what extent? Second, and even more important, if we assume that such a transformation has to some degree occurred, why exactly did it happen, and can it be reversed? Inequalities with Respect to Labor and Capital To answer these questions, I must first introduce certain basic ideas and the fundamental patterns of income and wealth inequality in different societies at different times. I showed in Part One that income can always be expressed as the sum of income from labor and income from capital. Wages are one form of income from labor, and to simplify the exposition I will sometimes speak of wage inequality when I mean inequality of income from labor more generally. To be sure, income from labor also includes income from nonwage labor, which for a long time played a crucial role and still plays a nonnegligible role today. Income from capital can also take different forms: it includes all income derived from the ownership of capital independent of any labor and regardless of its legal classification (rents, dividends, interest, royalties, profits, capital gains, etc.). By definition, in all societies, income inequality is the result of adding up these two components: inequality of income from labor and inequality of income from capital. The more unequally distributed each of these two components is, the greater the total inequality. In the abstract, it is perfectly possible to imagine a society in which inequality with respect to labor is high and inequality 3 4 with respect to capital is low, or vice versa, as well as a society in which both components are highly unequal or highly egalitarian. The third decisive factor is the relation between these two dimensions of inequality: to what extent do individuals with high income from labor also enjoy high income from capital? Technically speaking, this relation is a statistical correlation, and the greater the correlation, the greater the total inequality, all other things being equal. In practice, the correlation in question is often low or negative in societies in which inequality with respect to capital is so great that the owners of capital do not need to work (for example, Jane Austen's heroes usually eschew any profession). How do things stand today, and how will they stand in the future? Note, too, that inequality of income from capital may be greater than inequality of capital itself, if individuals with large fortunes somehow manage to obtain a higher return than those with modest to middling fortunes. This mechanism can be a powerful multiplier of inequality, and this is especially true in the century that has just begun. In the simple case where the average rate of return is the same at all levels of the wealth hierarchy, then by definition the two inequalities coincide. When analyzing the unequal distribution of income, it is essential to carefully distinguish these various aspects and components of inequality, first for normative and moral reasons (the justification of inequality is quite different for income from labor, from inherited wealth, and from differential returns on capital), and second, because the economic, social, and political mechanisms capable of explaining the observed evolutions are totally distinct. In the case of unequal incomes from labor, these mechanisms include the supply of and demand for different skills, the state of the educational system, and the various rules and institutions that affect the operation of the labor market and the determination of wages. In the case of unequal incomes from capital, the most important processes involve savings and investment behavior, laws governing gift-giving and inheritance, and the operation of real estate and financial markets. The statistical measures of income inequality that one finds in the writings of economists as well as in public debate are all too often synthetic indices, such as the Gini coefficient, which mix very different things, such as inequality with respect to labor and capital, so that it is impossible to distinguish clearly among the multiple dimensions of inequality and the various mechanisms at work. By contrast, I will try to distinguish these things as precisely as possible. Capital: Always More Unequally Distributed Than Labor The first regularity we observe when we try to measure income inequality in practice is that inequality with respect to capital is always greater than inequality with respect to labor. The distribution of capital ownership (and of income from capital) is always more concentrated than the distribution of income from labor. Two points need to be clarified at once. First, we find this regularity in all countries in all periods for which data are available, without exception, and the magnitude of the phenomenon is always quite striking. To give a preliminary idea of the order of magnitude in question, the upper 10 percent of the labor income distribution generally receives 25–30 percent of total labor income, whereas the top 10 percent of the capital income distribution always owns more than 50 percent of all wealth (and in some societies as much as 90 percent). Even more strikingly, perhaps, the bottom 50 percent of the wage distribution always receives a significant share of total labor income (generally between onequarter and one-third, or approximately as much as the top 10 percent), whereas the bottom 50 percent of the wealth distribution owns nothing at all, or almost nothing (always less than 10 percent and generally less than 5 percent of total wealth, or one-tenth as much as the wealthiest 10 percent). Inequalities with respect to labor usually seem mild, moderate, and almost reasonable (to the extent that inequality can be reasonable—this point should not be overstated). In comparison, inequalities with respect to capital are always extreme. Second, this regularity is by no means foreordained, and its existence tells us something important about the nature of the economic and social processes that shape the dynamics of capital accumulation and the distribution of wealth. Indeed, it is not difficult to think of mechanisms that would lead to a distribution of wealth more egalitarian than the distribution of income from labor. For example, suppose that at a given point in time, labor incomes reflect not only permanent wage inequalities among different groups of workers (based on the skill level and hierarchical position of each group) but also short-term shocks (for instance: wages and working hours in different sectors might fluctuate considerably from year to year or over the course of an individual's career). Labor incomes would then be highly unequal in the short run, although this inequality would diminish if measured over a long period (say ten years rather than one, or even over the lifetime of an individual, although this is rarely done because of the lack of long-term data). A longer-term perspective would be ideal for studying the true inequalities of opportunity and status that are the subject of Vautrin's lecture but are unfortunately often quite difficult to measure. In a world with large short-term wage fluctuations, the main reason for accumulating wealth might be precautionary (as a reserve against a possible negative shock to income), in which case inequality of wealth would be smaller than wage inequality. For example, inequality of wealth might be of the same order of magnitude as the permanent inequality of wage income (measured over the length of an individual career) and therefore significantly lower than the instantaneous wage inequality (measured at a given point in time). All of this is logically possible but clearly not very relevant to the real world, since inequality of wealth is always and everywhere much greater than inequality of income from labor. Although precautionary saving in anticipation of short-term shocks does indeed exist in the real world, it is clearly not the primary explanation for the observed accumulation and distribution of wealth. We can also imagine mechanisms that would imply an inequality of wealth comparable in magnitude to the inequality of income from labor. Specifically, if wealth is accumulated primarily for life-cycle reasons (saving for retirement, say), as Modigliani reasoned, then everyone would be expected to accumulate a stock of capital more or less proportional to his or her wage level in order to maintain approximately the same standard of living (or the same proportion thereof) after retirement. In that case, inequality of wealth would be a simple translation in time of inequality of income from labor and would as such have only limited importance, since the only real source of social inequality would be inequality with respect to labor. Once again, such a mechanism is theoretically plausible, and its real-world role is of some significance, especially in aging societies. In quantitative terms, however, it is not the primary mechanism at work. Life-cycle saving cannot explain the very highly concentrated ownership of capital we observe in practice, any more than precautionary saving can. To be sure, older individuals are certainly richer on average than younger ones. But the concentration of wealth is actually nearly as great within each age cohort as it is for the population as a whole. In other words, and contrary to a widespread belief, intergenerational warfare has not replaced class warfare. The very high concentration of capital is explained mainly by the importance of inherited wealth and its cumulative effects: for example, it is easier to save if you inherit an apartment and do not have to pay rent. The fact that the return on capital often takes on extreme values also plays a significant role in this dynamic process. In the remainder of Part Three, I examine these various mechanisms in greater detail and consider how their relative importance has evolved in time and space. At this stage, I note simply that the magnitude of inequality of wealth, both in absolute terms and relative to inequality of income from labor—points toward certain mechanisms rather than others. Inequalities and Concentration: Some Orders of Magnitude Before analyzing the historical evolutions that can be observed in different countries, it will be useful to give a more precise account of the characteristic orders of magnitude of inequality with respect to labor and capital. The goal is to familiarize the reader with numbers and notions such as deciles, centiles, and the like, which may seem somewhat technical and even distasteful to some but are actually quite useful for analyzing and understanding changes in the structure of inequality in different societies—provided we use them correctly. To that end, I have charted in Tables 7.1–3 the distributions actually observed in various countries at various times. The figures indicated are approximate and deliberately rounded off but at least give us a preliminary idea of what the terms "low," "medium," and "high" inequality mean today and have meant in the past, with respect to both income from labor and ownership of capital, and finally with respect to total income (the sum of income from labor and income from capital). For example, with respect to inequality of income from labor, we find that in the most egalitarian societies, such as the Scandinavian countries in the 1970s and 1980s (inequalities have increased in northern Europe since then, but these countries nevertheless remain the least inegalitarian), the distribution is roughly as follows. Looking at the entire adult population, we see that the 10 percent receiving the highest incomes from labor claim a little more than 20 percent of the total income fromlabor (and in practice this means essentially wages); the least well paid 50 percent get about 35 percent of the total; and the 40 percent in the middle therefore receive roughly 45 percent of the total . This is not perfect equality, for in that case each group should receive the equivalent of its share of the population (the best paid 10 percent should get exactly 10 percent of the income, and the worst paid 50 percent should get 50 percent). But the inequality we see here is not too extreme, at least in comparison to what we observe in other countries or at other times, and it is not too extreme especially when compared with what we find almost everywhere for the ownership of capital, even in the Scandinavian countries.

In order to have a clear idea of what these figures really mean, we need to relate distributions expressed as percentages of total income to the paychecks that flesh-and-blood workers actually receive as well as to the fortunes in real estate and financial assets owned by the people who actually make up these wealth hierarchies. Concretely, if the best paid 10 percent receive 20 percent of total wages, then it follows mathematically that each person in this group earns on average twice the average pay in the country in question. Similarly, if the least well paid 50 percent receive 35 percent of total wages, it follows that each person in this group earns on average 70 percent of the average wage. And if the middle 40 percent receive 45 percent of the total wage, this means that the average wage of this group is slightly higher than the average pay for society as a whole (45/40 of the average, to be precise). For example, if the average pay in a country is 2,000 euros per month, then this distribution implies that the top 10 percent earn 4,000 euros a month on average, the bottom 50 percent 1,400 euros a 6 month, and the middle 40 percent 2,250 a month. This intermediate group may be regarded as a vast "middle class" whose standard of living is determined by the average wage of the society in question.

I introduce these terms purely for illustrative purposes, to pin down my ideas, but in fact they play virtually no role in the analysis, and I might just as well have called them "Class A," "Class B," and "Class C." In political debate, however, such terminological issues are generally far from innocent. The way the population is divided up usually reflects an implicit or explicit position concerning the justice and legitimacy of the amount of income or wealth claimed by a particular group. For example, some people use the term "middle class" very broadly to encompass individuals who clearly fall within the upper decile (that is, the top 10 percent) of the social hierarchy and who may even be quite close to the upper centile (the top 1 percent). Generally, the purpose of such a broad definition of the middle class is to insist that even though such individuals dispose of resources considerably above the average for the society in question, they nevertheless retain a certain proximity to the average: in other words, the point is to say that such individuals are not privileged and fully deserve the indulgence of the government, particularly in regard to taxes. Other commentators reject any notion of "middle class" and prefer to describe the social structure as consisting of just two groups: "the people," who constitute the vast minority, and a tiny "elite" or "upper class." Such a description may be accurate for some societies, or it may be applicable to certain political or historical contexts. For example, in France in 1789, it is generally estimated that the aristocracy represented 1–2 percent of the population, the clergy less than 1 percent, and the "Third Estate," meaning (under the political system of the Ancien Régime) all the rest, from peasantry to bourgeoisie, more than 97 percent. It is not my purpose to police dictionaries or linguistic usage. When it comes to designating social groups, everyone is right and wrong at the same time. Everyone has good reasons for using certain terms but is wrong to denigrate the terms used by others. My definition of "middle class" (as the "middle" 40 percent) is highly contestable, since the income (or wealth) of everyone in the group is, by construction, above the median for the society in question. One might equally well choose to divide society into three thirds and call the middle third the "middle class." Still, the definition I have given seems to me to correspond more closely to common usage: the expression "middle class" is generally used to refer to people who are doing distinctly better than the bulk of the population yet still a long way from the true "elite." Yet all such designations are open to challenge, and there is no need for me to take a position on this delicate issue, which is not just linguistic but also political. The truth is that any representation of inequality that relies on a small number of categories is doomed to be crudely schematic, since the underlying social reality is always a continuous distribution. At any given level of wealth or income there is always a certain number of flesh-andblood individuals, and the number of such individuals varies slowly and gradually in accordance with the shape of the distribution in the society in question. There is never a discontinuous break between 6 7 social classes or between "people" and "elite." For that reason, my analysis is based entirely on statistical concepts such as deciles (top 10 percent, middle 40 percent, lower 50 percent, etc.), which are defined in exactly the same way in different societies. This allows me to make rigorous and objective comparisons across time and space without denying the intrinsic complexity of each particular society or the fundamentally continuous structure of social inequality. Class Struggle or Centile Struggle? My fundamental goal is to compare the structure of inequality in societies remote from one another in time and space, societies that are very different a priori, and in particular societies that use totally different words and concepts to refer to the social groups that compose them. The concepts of deciles and centiles are rather abstract and undoubtedly lack a certain poetry. It is easier for most people to identify with groups with which they are familiar: peasants or nobles, proletarians or bourgeois, office workers or top managers, waiters or traders. But the beauty of deciles and centiles is precisely that they enable us to compare inequalities that would otherwise be incomparable, using a common language that should in principle be acceptable to everyone. When necessary, we will break down our groups even more finely, using centiles or even thousandths to register more precisely the continuous character of social inequality. Specifically, in every society, even the most egalitarian, the upper decile is truly a world unto itself. It includes some people whose income is just two or three times greater than the mean and others whose resources are ten or twenty times greater, if not more. To start with, it is always enlightening to break the top decile down into two subgroups: the upper centile (which we might call the "dominant class" for the sake of concreteness, without claiming that this term is better than any other) and the remaining nine centiles (which we might call the "wealthy class" or "well-to-do"). For example, if we look at the case where inequality of income from labor is relatively low (think Scandinavia), represented in with 20 percent of wages going to the best paid 10 percent of workers, we find that the share going to the top 1 percent is typically on the order of 5 percent of total wages. This means that the top 1 percent of earners make on average five times the mean wage, or 10,000 euros per month, in a society in which the average wage is 2,000 euros per month. In other words, the best paid 10 percent earn 4,000 euros a month on average, but within that group the top 1 percent earn an average of 10,000 euros a month (and the next 9 percent earn on average 3,330 euros a month). If we break this down even further and looked at the top thousandth (the best paid 0.1 percent) in the top centile, we find individuals earning tens of thousands of euros a month and a few earning hundreds of thousands, even in the Scandinavian countries in the 1970s and 1980s. Of course there would not be many such people, so their weight in the sum total of all wages would be relatively small. Thus to judge the inequality of a society, it is not enough to observe that some individuals earn very high incomes. For example, to say that the "income scale goes from 1 to 10" or even "1 to 100" does not actually tell us very much. We also need to know how many people earn the incomes at each level. The share of income (or wealth) going to the top decile or centile is a useful index for judging how unequal a society is, because it reflects not just the existence of extremely high incomes or extremely large fortunes but also the number of individuals who enjoy such rewards. The top centile is a particularly interesting group to study in the context of my historical investigation. Although it constitutes (by definition) a very small minority of the population, it is nevertheless far larger than the superelites of a few dozen or hundred individuals on whom attention is sometimes focused (such as the "200 families" of France, to use the designation widely applied in the interwar years to the 200 largest stockholders of the Banque de France, or the "400 richest Americans" or similar rankings established by magazines like Forbes). In a country of almost 65 million people such as France in 2013, of whom some 50 million are adults, the top centile comprises some 500,000 people. In a country of 320 million like the United States, of whom 260 million are adults, the top centile consists of 2.6 million individuals. These are numerically quite large groups who inevitably stand out in society, especially when the individuals included in them tend to live in the same cities and even to congregate in the same neighborhoods. In every country the upper centile occupies a prominent place in the social landscape and not just in the income distribution. Thus in every society, whether France in 1789 (when 1–2 percent of the population belonged to the aristocracy) or the United States in 2011 (when the Occupy Wall Street movement aimed its criticismat the richest 1 percent of the population), the top centile is a large enough group to exert a significant influence on both the social landscape and the political and economic order. This shows why deciles and centiles are so interesting to study. How could one hope to compare inequalities in societies as different as France in 1789 and the United States in 2011 other than by carefully examining deciles and centiles and estimating the shares of national wealth and income going to each? To be sure, this procedure will not allow us to eliminate every problem or settle every question, but at least it will allow us to say something—and that is far better than not being able to say anything at all. We can therefore try to determine whether "the 1 percent" had more power under Louis XVI or under George Bush and Barack Obama. To return for a moment to the Occupy Wall Street movement, what it shows is that the use of a common terminology, and in particular the concept of the "top centile," though it may at first glance seem somewhat abstract, can be helpful in revealing the spectacular growth of inequality and may therefore serve as a useful tool for social interpretation and criticism. Even mass social movements can avail themselves of such a tool to develop unusual mobilizing themes, such as "We are the 99 percent!" This might seem surprising at first sight, until we remember that the title of the famous pamphlet that Abbé Sieyès published in January 1789 was "What Is the Third Estate?" I should also make it clear that the hierarchies (and therefore centiles and deciles) of income are not the same as those of wealth. The top 10 percent or bottom 50 percent of the labor income distribution are not the same people who constitute the top 10 percent or bottom 50 percent of the wealth distribution. The "1 percent" who earn the most are not the same as the "1 percent" who own the most. Deciles and centiles are defined separately for income from labor, ownership of capital, and total income (from both labor and capital), with the third being a synthesis of the first two dimensions and thus defining a composite social hierarchy. It is always essential to be clear about which hierarchy one is referring to. In traditional societies, the correlation between the two dimensions was often negative (because people with large fortunes did not work and were therefore at the bottom of the labor income hierarchy). In modern societies, the correlation is generally positive but never perfect (the coefficient of correlation is always less than one). For example, many people 8 belong to the upper class in terms of labor income but to the lower class in terms of wealth, and vice versa. Social inequality is multidimensional, just like political conflict. Note, finally, that the income and wealth distributions described in and analyzed in this and subsequent chapters are in all cases "primary" distributions, meaning before taxes. Depending on whether the tax system (and the public services and transfer payments it finances) is "progressive" or "regressive" (meaning that it weighs more or less heavily on different groups depending on whether they stand high or low in the income or wealth hierarchy), the after-tax distribution may be more or less egalitarian than the before-tax distribution. I will come back to this in

Part Four, along with many other questions related to redistribution. At this stage only the beforetax distribution requires consideration. Inequalities with Respect to Labor: Moderate Inequality? To return to the question of orders of magnitude of inequality: To what extent are inequalities of income from labor moderate, reasonable, or even no longer an issue today? It is true that inequalities with respect to labor are always much smaller than inequalities with respect to capital. It would be quite wrong, however, to neglect them, first because income from labor generally accounts for twothirds to three-quarters of national income, and second because there are quite substantial differences between countries in the distribution of income from labor, which suggests that public policies and national differences can have major consequences for these inequalities and for the living conditions of large numbers of people. In countries where income from labor is most equally distributed, such as the Scandinavian countries between 1970 and 1990, the top 10 percent of earners receive about 20 percent of total wages and the bottom 50 percent about 35 percent. In countries where wage inequality is average, including most European countries (such as France and Germany) today, the first group claims 25–30 percent of total wages, and the second around 30 percent. And in the most inegalitarian countries, such as the United States in the early 2010s (where, as will emerge later, income from labor is about as unequally distributed as has ever been observed anywhere), the top decile gets 35 percent of the total, whereas the bottom half gets only 25 percent. In other words, the equilibrium between the two groups is almost completely reversed. In the most egalitarian countries, the bottom 50 percent receive nearly twice as much total income as the top 10 percent (which some will say is still too little, since the former group is five times as large as the latter), whereas in the most inegalitarian countries the bottom 50 percent receive one-third less than the top group. If the growing concentration of income from labor that has been observed in the United States over the last few decades were to continue, the bottom 50 percent could earn just half as much in total compensation as the top 10 percent by 2030.

Obviously there is no certainty that this evolution will in fact continue, but the point illustrates the fact that recent changes in the income distribution have by no means been painless. In concrete terms, if the average wage is 2,000 euros a month, the egalitarian (Scandinavian) distribution corresponds to 4,000 euros a month for the top 10 percent of earners (and 10,000 for the top 1 percent), 2,250 a month for the 40 percent in the middle, and 1,400 a month for the bottom 50 percent, where the more inegalitarian (US) distribution corresponds to a markedly steeper hierarchy: 7,000 euros a month for the top 10 percent (and 24,000 for the top 1 percent), 2,000 for the middle 40 9 percent, and just 1,000 for the bottom 50 percent. For the least-favored half of the population, the difference between the two income distributions is therefore far from negligible: if a person earns 1,400 euros a month instead of 1,000—40 percent additional income—even leaving taxes and transfers aside, the consequences for lifestyle choices, housing, vacation opportunities, and money to spend on projects, children, and so on are considerable. In most countries, moreover, women are in fact significantly overrepresented in the bottom 50 percent of earners, so that these large differences between countries reflect in part differences in the male-female wage gap, which is smaller in northern Europe than elsewhere. The gap between the two distributions is also significant for the top-earning group: a person who all his or her life earns 7,000 euros a month rather than 4,000 (or, even better, 24,000 instead of 10,000), will not spend money on the same things and will have greater power not only over what he or she buys but also over other people: for instance, this person can hire less well paid individuals to serve his or her needs. If the trend observed in the United States were to continue, then by 2030 the top 10 percent of earners will be making 9,000 euros a month (and the top 1 percent, 34,000 euros), the middle 40 percent will earn 1,750, and the bottom 50 percent just 800 a month. The top 10 percent could therefore use a small portion of their incomes to hire many of the bottom 50 percent as domestic servants. Clearly, then, the same mean wage is compatible with very different distributions of income fromlabor, which can result in very disparate social and economic realities for different social groups. In some cases, these inequalities may give rise to conflict. It is therefore important to understand the economic, social, and political forces that determine the degree of labor income inequality in different societies. Inequalities with Respect to Capital: Extreme Inequality Although inequality with respect to income from labor is sometimes seen—incorrectly—as moderate inequality that no longer gives rise to conflict, this is largely a consequence of comparing it with the distribution of capital ownership, which is extremely inegalitarian everywhere (see Table 7.2). In the societies where wealth is most equally distributed (once again, the Scandinavian countries in the 1970s and 1980s), the richest 10 percent own around 50 percent of national wealth or even a bit more, somewhere between 50 and 60 percent, if one properly accounts for the largest fortunes. Currently, in the early 2010s, the richest 10 percent own around 60 percent of national wealth in most European countries, and in particular in France, Germany, Britain, and Italy. The most striking fact is no doubt that in all these societies, half of the population own virtually nothing: the poorest 50 percent invariably own less than 10 percent of national wealth, and generally less than 5 percent. In France, according to the latest available data (for 2010–2011), the richest 10 percent command 62 percent of total wealth, while the poorest 50 percent own only 4 percent. In the United States, the most recent survey by the Federal Reserve, which covers the same years, indicates that the top decile own 72 percent of America's wealth, while the bottom half claim just 2 percent. Note, however, that this source, like most surveys in which wealth is self-reported, underestimates the largest fortunes. As noted, moreover, it is also important to add that we find the same concentration of wealth within each age cohort. 10 11 12 Ultimately, inequalities of wealth in the countries that are most egalitarian in that regard (such as the Scandinavian countries in the 1970s and 1980s) appear to be considerably greater than wage inequalities in the countries that are most inegalitarian with respect to wages.

To my knowledge, no society has ever existed in which ownership of capital can reasonably be described as "mildly" inegalitarian, by which I mean a distribution in which the poorest half of society would own a significant share (say, one-fifth to onequarter) of total wealth. Optimism is not forbidden, however, so I have indicated in a virtual example of a possible distribution of wealth in which inequality would be "low," or at any rate lower than it is in Scandinavia (where it is "medium"), Europe ("medium-to-high"), or the United States ("high"). Of course, how one might go about establishing such an "ideal society"—assuming that such low inequality of wealth is indeed a desirable goal—remains to be seen.

As in the case of wage inequality, it is important to have a good grasp of exactly what these wealth figures mean. Imagine a society in which average net wealth is 200,000 euros per adult, which is roughly the case today in the richest European countries. As noted in Part Two, this private wealth can be divided into two roughly equal parts: real estate on the one hand and financial and business assets on the other (these include bank deposits, savings plans, portfolios of stocks and bonds, life insurance, pension funds, etc., net of debts). Of course these are average figures, and there are large variations between countries and enormous variations between individuals.

If the poorest 50 percent own 5 percent of total wealth, then by definition each member of that group owns on average the equivalent of 10 percent of the average individual wealth of society as a whole. In the example in the previous paragraph, it follows that each person among the poorest 50 percent possesses on average a net wealth of 20,000 euros. This is not nothing, but it is very little compared with the wealth of the rest of society. Concretely, in such a society, the poorest half of the population will generally comprise a large number of people—typically a quarter of the population—with no wealth at all or perhaps a few thousand euros at most. Indeed, a nonnegligible number of people—perhaps one-twentieth to onetenth of the population—will have slightly negative net wealth (their debts exceed their assets). Others will own small amounts of wealth up to about 60,000 or 70,000 euros or perhaps a bit more. This range of situations, including the existence of a large number of people with very close to zero absolute wealth, results in an average wealth of about 20,000 euros for the poorest half of the population. Some of these people may own real estate that remains heavily indebted, while others may possess very small nest eggs. Most, however, are renters whose only wealth consists of a few thousand euros of savings in a checking or savings account. If we included durable goods such as cars, furniture, appliances, and the like in wealth, then the average wealth of the poorest 50 percent would increase to no more than 30,000 or 40,000 euros. For this half of the population, the very notions of wealth and capital are relatively abstract. For millions of people, "wealth" amounts to little more than a few weeks' wages in a checking account or low-interest savings account, a car, and a few pieces of furniture. The inescapable reality is this: wealth is so concentrated that a large segment of society is virtually unaware of its existence, so that some people imagine that it belongs to surreal or mysterious entities. That is why it is so essential to 13 14 15 16 17 study capital and its distribution in a methodical, systematic way. At the other end of the scale, the richest 10 percent own 60 percent of total wealth. It therefore follows that each member of this group owns on average 6 times the average wealth of the society in question. In the example, with an average wealth of 200,000 euros per adult, each of the richest 10 percent therefore owns on average the equivalent of 1.2 million euros. The upper decile of the wealth distribution is itself extremely unequal, even more so than the upper decile of the wage distribution. When the upper decile claims about 60 percent of total wealth, as is the case in most European countries today, the share of the upper centile is generally around 25 percent and that of the next 9 percent of the population is about 35 percent. The members of the first group are therefore on average 25 times as rich as the average member of society, while the members of the second group are barely 4 times richer. Concretely, in the example, the average wealth of the top 10 percent is 1.2 million euros each, with 5 million euros each for the top 1 percent and a little less than 800,000 each for the next 9 percent. In addition, the composition of wealth varies widely within this group. Nearly everyone in the top decile owns his or her own home, but the importance of real estate decreases sharply as one moves higher in the wealth hierarchy. In the "9 percent" group, at around 1 million euros, real estate accounts for half of total wealth and for some individuals more than three-quarters. In the top centile, by contrast, financial and business assets clearly predominate over real estate. In particular, shares of stock or partnerships constitute nearly the totality of the largest fortunes. Between 2 and 5 million euros, the share of real estate is less than one-third; above 5 million euros, it falls below 20 percent; above 10 million euros, it is less than 10 percent and wealth consists primarily of stock. Housing is the favorite investment of the middle class and moderately well-to-do, but true wealth always consists primarily of financial and business assets. Between the poorest 50 percent (who own 5 percent of total wealth, or an average of 20,000 euros each in the example) and the richest 10 percent (who own 60 percent of total wealth, or an average of 1.2 million euros each) lies the middle 40 percent: this "middle class of wealth" owns 35 percent of total national wealth, which means that their average net wealth is fairly close to the average for society as a whole—in the example, it comes to exactly 175,000 euros per adult. Within this vast group, where individual wealth ranges from barely 100,000 euros to more than 400,000, a key role is often played by ownership of a primary residence and the way it is acquired and paid for. Sometimes, in addition to a home, there is also a substantial amount of savings. For example, a net capital of 200,000 euros may consist of a house valued at 250,000 euros, from which an outstanding mortgage balance of 100,000 euros must be deducted, together with savings of 50,000 euros invested in a life insurance policy or retirement savings account. When the mortgage is fully paid off, net wealth in this case will rise to 300,000 euros, or even more if the savings account has grown in the meantime. This is a typical trajectory in the middle class of the wealth hierarchy, who are richer than the poorest 50 percent (who own practically nothing) but poorer than the richest 10 percent (who own much more). A Major Innovation: The Patrimonial Middle Class Make no mistake: the growth of a true "patrimonial (or propertied) middle class" was the principal structural transformation of the distribution of wealth in the developed countries in the twentieth century.

Unsurprisingly, the level of inequality of total income falls between inequality of income from labor and inequality of ownership of capital. Note, too, that inequality of total income is closer to inequality of income from labor than to inequality of capital, which comes as no surprise, since income from labor generally accounts for two-thirds to three-quarters of total national income. Concretely, the top decile of the income hierarchy received about 25 percent of national income in the egalitarian societies of Scandinavia in the 1970s and 1980s (it was 30 percent in Germany and France at that time and is more than 35 percent now). In more inegalitarian societies, the top decile claimed as much as 50 percent of national income (with about 20 percent going to the top centile). This was true in France and Britain during the Ancien Régime as well as the Belle Époque and is true in the United States today. Is it possible to imagine societies in which the concentration of income is much greater? Probably not. If, for example, the top decile appropriates 90 percent of each year's output (and the top centile took 50 percent just for itself, as in the case of wealth), a revolution will likely occur, unless some peculiarly effective repressive apparatus exists to keep it from happening. When it comes to the ownership of capital, such a high degree of concentration is already a source of powerful political tensions, which are often difficult to reconcile with universal suffrage. Yet such capital concentration might be tenable if the income from capital accounts for only a small part of national income: perhaps one-fourth to one-third, or sometimes a bit more, as in the Ancien Régime (which made the extreme concentration of wealth at that time particularly oppressive). But if the same level of inequality applies to the totality of national income, it is hard to imagine that those at the bottom will accept the situation permanently. That said, there are no grounds for asserting that the upper decile can never claim more than 50 percent of national income or that a country's economy would collapse if this symbolic threshold were crossed. In fact, the available historical data are far from perfect, and it is not out of the question that this symbolic limit has already been exceeded. In particular, it is possible that under the Ancien Régime, right up to the eve of the French Revolution, the top decile did take more than 50 percent and even as much as 60 percent or perhaps slightly more of national income. More generally, this may have been the case in other traditional rural societies. Indeed, whether such extreme inequality is or is not sustainable depends not only on the effectiveness of the repressive apparatus but also, and perhaps primarily, on the effectiveness of the apparatus of justification. If inequalities are seen as justified, say because they seem to be a consequence of a choice by the rich to work harder or more efficiently than the poor, or because preventing the rich from earning more would inevitably harm the worst-off members of society, then it is perfectly possible for the concentration of income to set new historical records. That is why I indicate in Table 7.3 that the United States may set a new record around 2030 if inequality of income from labor—and to a lesser extent inequality of ownership of capital—continue to increase as they have done in recent decades. The top decile would them claim about 60 percent of national income, while the bottom half would get barely 15 percent. I want to insist on this point: the key issue is the justification of inequalities rather than their magnitude as such. That is why it is essential to analyze the structure of inequality. In this respect, the principal message of Tables 7.1–3 is surely that there are two different ways for a society to achieve a very unequal distribution of total income (around 50 percent for the top decile and 20 percent for the top centile). The first of these two ways of achieving such high inequality is through a "hyperpatrimonial society" (or "society of rentiers"): a society in which inherited wealth is very important and where the concentration of wealth attains extreme levels (with the upper decile owning typically 90 percent of all wealth, with 50 percent belonging to the upper centile alone). The total income hierarchy is then dominated by very high incomes from capital, especially inherited capital. This is the pattern we see in Ancien Régime France and in Europe during the Belle Époque, with on the whole minor variations. We need to understand how such structures of ownership and inequality emerged and persisted and to what extent they belong to the past—unless of course they are also pertinent to the future. The second way of achieving such high inequality is relatively new. It was largely created by the United States over the past few decades. Here we see that a very high level of total income inequality can be the result of a "hypermeritocratic society" (or at any rate a society that the people at the top like to describe as hypermeritocratic). One might also call this a "society of superstars" (or perhaps "supermanagers," a somewhat different characterization). In other words, this is a very inegalitarian society, but one in which the peak of the income hierarchy is dominated by very high incomes fromlabor rather than by inherited wealth. I want to be clear that at this stage I am not making a judgment about whether a society of this kind really deserves to be characterized as "hypermeritocratic." It is hardly surprising that the winners in such a society would wish to describe the social hierarchy in this way, and sometimes they succeed in convincing some of the losers. For present purposes, however, hypermeritocracy is not a hypothesis but one possible conclusion of the analysis—bearing in mind that the opposite conclusion is equally possible. I will analyze in what follows how far the rise of labor income inequality in the United States has obeyed a "meritocratic" logic (insofar as it is possible to answer such a complex normative question). At this point it will suffice to note that the stark contrast I have drawn here between two types of hyperinegalitarian society—a society of rentiers and a society of supermanagers—is naïve and overdrawn. The two types of inequality can coexist: there is no reason why a person can't be both a supermanager and a rentier—and the fact that the concentration of wealth is currently much higher in the United States than in Europe suggests that this may well be the case in the United States today. And of course there is nothing to prevent the children of supermanagers from becoming rentiers. In practice, we find both logics at work in every society. Nevertheless, there is more than one way of achieving the same level of inequality, and what primarily characterizes the United States at the moment is a record level of inequality of income from labor (probably higher than in any other society at any time in the past, anywhere in the world, including societies in which skill disparities were extremely large) together with a level of inequality of wealth less extreme than the levels observed in traditional societies or in Europe in the period 1900–1910. It is therefore essential to understand the conditions under which each of these two logics could develop, while keeping in mind that they may complement each other in the century ahead and combine their effects. If this happens, the future could hold in store a new world of inequality more extreme than any that preceded it. Problems of Synthetic Indices Before turning to a country-by-country examination of the historical evolution of inequality in order to answer the questions posed above, several methodological issues remain to be discussed. In particular, Tables 7.1–3 include indications of the Gini coefficients of the various distributions considered. The Gini coefficient—named for the Italian statistician Corrado Gini

(1884–1965)—is one of the more commonly used synthetic indices of inequality, frequently found in official reports and public debate. By construction, it ranges from 0 to 1: it is equal to 0 in case of complete equality and to 1 when inequality is absolute, that is, when a very tiny group owns all available resources. In practice, the Gini coefficient varies from roughly 0.2 to 0.4 in the distributions of labor income observed in actual societies, from 0.6 to 0.9 for observed distributions of capital ownership, and from 0.3 to 0.5 for total income inequality. In Scandinavia in the 1970s and 1980s, the Gini coefficient of the labor income distribution was 0.19, not far from absolute equality. Conversely, the wealth distribution in Belle Époque Europe exhibited a Gini coefficient of 0.85, not far from absolute inequality. These coefficients—and there are others, such as the Theil index—are sometimes useful, but they raise many problems. They claim to summarize in a single numerical index all that a distribution can tell us about inequality—the inequality between the bottom and the middle of the hierarchy as well as between the middle and the top or between the top and the very top. This is very simple and appealing at first glance but inevitably somewhat misleading. Indeed, it is impossible to summarize a multidimensional reality with a unidimensional index without unduly simplifying matters and mixing up things that should not be treated together. The social reality and economic and political significance of inequality are very different at different levels of the distribution, and it is important to analyze these separately. In addition, Gini coefficients and other synthetic indices tend to confuse inequality in regard to labor with inequality in regard to capital, even though the economic mechanisms at work, as well as the normative justifications of inequality, are very different in the two 21 22 cases. For all these reasons, it seemed to me far better to analyze inequalities in terms of distribution tables indicating the shares of various deciles and centiles in total income and total wealth rather than using synthetic indices such as the Gini coefficient. Distribution tables are also valuable because they force everyone to take note of the income and wealth levels of the various social groups that make up the existing hierarchy. These levels are expressed in cash terms (or as a percentage of average income and wealth levels in the country concerned) rather than by way of artificial statistical measures that can be difficult to interpret. Distribution tables allow us to have a more concrete and visceral understanding of social inequality, as well as an appreciation of the data available to study these issues and the limits of those data. By contrast, statistical indices such as the Gini coefficient give an abstract and sterile view of inequality, which makes it difficult for people to grasp their position in the contemporary hierarchy (always a useful exercise, particularly when one belongs to the upper centiles of the distribution and tends to forget it, as is often the case with economists). Indices often obscure the fact that there are anomalies or inconsistencies in the underlying data, or that data from other countries or other periods are not directly comparable (because, for example, the tops of the distribution have been truncated or because income from capital is omitted for some countries but not others). Working with distribution tables forces us to be more consistent and transparent. The Chaste Veil of Of icial Publications For similar reasons, caution is in order when using indices such as the interdecile ratios often cited in official reports on inequality from the OECD or national statistical agencies. The most frequently used interdecile ratio is the P90/P10, that is, the ratio between the ninetieth percentile of the income distribution and the tenth percentile. For example, if one needs to earn more than 5,000 euros a month to belong to the top 10 percent of the income distribution and less than 1,000 euros a month to belong to the bottom 10 percent, then the P90/P10 ratio is 5. Such indices can be useful. It is always valuable to have more information about the complete shape of the distribution in question. One should bear in mind, however, that by construction these ratios totally ignore the evolution of the distribution beyond the ninetieth percentile. Concretely, no matter what the P90/P10 ratio may be, the top decile of the income or wealth distribution may have 20 percent of the total (as in the case of Scandinavian incomes in the 1970s and 1980s) or 50 percent (as in the case of US incomes in the 2010s) or 90 percent (as in the case of European wealth in the Belle Époque). We will not learn any of this by consulting the publications of the international organizations or national statistical agencies who compile these statistics, however, because they usually focus on indices that deliberately ignore the top end of the distribution and give no indication of income or wealth beyond the ninetieth percentile. This practice is generally justified on the grounds that the available data are "imperfect." This is true, but the difficulties can be overcome by using adequate sources, as the historical data collected (with limited means) in the World Top Incomes Database (WTID) show. This work has begun, slowly, to change the way things are done. Indeed, the methodological decision to ignore the top end is hardly neutral: the official reports of national and international agencies are supposed to informpublic debate about the distribution of income and wealth, but in practice they often give an 23 artificially rosy picture of inequality. It is as if an official government report on inequalities in France in 1789 deliberately ignored everything above the ninetieth percentile—a group 5 to 10 times larger than the entire aristocracy of the day—on the grounds that it was too complex to say anything about. Such a chaste approach is all the more regrettable in that it inevitably feeds the wildest fantasies and tends to discredit official statistics and statisticians rather than calm social tensions. Conversely, interdecile ratios are sometimes quite high for largely artificial reasons. Take the distribution of capital ownership, for example: the bottom 50 percent of the distribution generally own next to nothing. Depending on how small fortunes are measured—for example, whether or not durable goods and debts are counted—one can come up with apparently quite different evaluations of exactly where the tenth percentile of the wealth hierarchy lies: for the same underlying social reality, one might put it at 100 euros, 1,000 euros, or even 10,000 euros, which in the end isn't all that different but can lead to very different interdecile ratios, depending on the country and the period, even though the bottom half of the wealth distribution owns less than 5 percent of total wealth. The same is only slightly less true of the labor income distribution: depending on how one chooses to treat replacement incomes and pay for short periods of work (for example, depending on whether one uses the average weekly, monthly, annual, or decadal income) one can come up with highly variable P10 thresholds (and therefore interdecile ratios), even though the bottom 50 percent of the labor income distribution actually draws a fairly stable share of the total income from labor. This is perhaps one of the main reasons why it is preferable to study distributions as I have presented them in Tables 7.1–3, that is, by emphasizing the shares of income and wealth claimed by different groups, particularly the bottom half and the top decile in each society, rather than the threshold levels defining given percentiles. The shares give a much more stable picture of reality than the interdecile ratios. Back to "Social Tables" and Political Arithmetic These, then, are my reasons for believing that the distribution tables I have been examining in this chapter are the best tool for studying the distribution of wealth, far better than synthetic indices and interdecile ratios. In addition, I believe that my approach is more consistent with national accounting methods. Now that national accounts for most countries enable us to measure national income and wealth every year (and therefore average income and wealth, since demographic sources provide easy access to population figures), the next step is naturally to break down these total income and wealth figures by decile and centile. Many reports have recommended that national accounts be improved and "humanized" in this way, but little progress has been made to date. A useful step in this direction would be a breakdown indicating the poorest 50 percent, the middle 40 percent, and the richest 10 percent. In particular, such an approach would allow any observer to see just how much the growth of domestic output and national income is or is not reflected in the income actually received by these different social groups. For instance, only by knowing the share going to the top decile can we determine the extent to which a disproportionate share of growth has been captured by the top end of the distribution. Neither a Gini coefficient nor an interdecile ratio permits such a clear and precise response to this question. 24 25 I will add, finally, that the distribution tables whose use I am recommending are in some waysfairly similar to the "social tables" that were in vogue in the eighteenth and early nineteenth centuries.First developed in Britain and France in the late seventeenth century, these social tables were widelyused, improved, and commented on in France during the Enlightenment: for example, in the celebratedarticle on "political arithmetic" in Diderot's Encyclopedia. From the earliest versions established byGregory King in 1688 to the more elaborate examples compiled by Expilly and Isnard on the eve ofthe French Revolution or by Peuchet, Colqhoun, and Blodget during the Napoleonic era, social tablesalways aimed to provide a comprehensive vision of the social structure: they indicated the number ofnobles, bourgeois, gentlemen, artisans, farmers, and so on along with their estimated income (andsometimes wealth); the same authors also compiled the earliest estimates of national income andwealth. There is, however, one essential difference between these tables and mine: the old socialtables used the social categories of their time and did not seek to ascertain the distribution of wealthor income by deciles and centiles. Nevertheless, social tables sought to portray the flesh-and-blood aspects of inequality byemphasizing the shares of national wealth held by different social groups (and, in particular, thevarious strata of the elite), and in this respect there are clear affinities with the approach I have takenhere. At the same time, social tables are remote in spirit from the sterile, atemporal statisticalmeasures of inequality such as those employed by Gini and Pareto, which were all too commonlyused in the twentieth century and tend to naturalize the distribution of wealth. The way one tries tomeasure inequality is never neutral.

9 798888 693926